THE MONTESSORI BOOK OF COORDINATION AND LIFE SKILLS

THE MONTESSORI BOOK OF COORDINATION AND LIFE SKILLS

RAISING
A CREATIVE
AND
CONFIDENT
CHILD

MAJA PITAMIC

First published in the USA and Canada in 2022 by Sourcebooks LLC
P.O. Box 4410, Naperville, Illinois 60567-4410
(630) 961-3900
sourcebooks.com

Conceived and produced by
Elwin Street Productions
10 Elwin Street
London E2 7BU

Some of the text from this book previously appeared in *Teach Me to Do It Myself* (2008). Illustrations by Isabel Alberdi

ISBN 978-1-4380-9000-9

[Cataloging-in-Publication Data is on file with the Library of Congress]

Printed and bound in the United Arab Emirates.

XX 10 9 8 7 6 5 4 3 2 1

Picture credits
pp. 5, 81 Alamy by ephotocorp; pp. 6, 83 Alamy by ephotocorp; pp. 7, 87 GettyImages by Marcy Maloy; pp. 7, 68, 95 GettyImages by PhotoAlto/Odilon Dimier; p. 8 Shutterstock by Dmitry Naumov; pp. 14, 25 GettyImages by Razvan Ciuca; pp. 14, 65 Alamy by Folio Images; pp. 14, 35 GettyImages by Ryan McVay; pp. 68, 96 Alamy by Age Fotostock; pp. 68, 91 GettyImages by ViewStock; p. 73 GettyImages by JR Carvey/Streetfly Studio; p. 103 Ellie Smith; p. 113 Shutterstock by Just Dance; pp. 116, 132 GettyImages by Jamie Grill; pp. 116, 141 GettyImages Jose Luis Pelaez Inc; pp. 116, 153 GettyImages by Tatiana Kolesnikova; p. 119 Alamy by Image Source / Alamy Stock Photo; p. 123 Alamy by ONOKY - Photononstop / Alamy Stock Photo; p. 127 Alamy by Tetra Images / Alamy Stock Photo; p. 130 GettyImages by MoMo Productions; p. 135 Shutterstock by Halfpoint; p. 136 Shutterstock by N_Belonogov; p. 138 GettyImages by Rubberball/Jessica Peterson; p. 143 Shutterstock by Pair Srinrat; p. 159 Alamy by Jozef Polc / Alamy Stock Photo; p. 161 GettyImages by thebang; p. 171 Shutterstock by LStockStudio

CONTENTS

1: Developing the Senses

2: Coordination

3: Life Skills

ABOUT MONTESSORI

Maria Montessori was born in Rome in 1870 and became the first female medical graduate of Rome University. In 1907, Montessori opened the first *Casa dei Bambini*, a school for children from slums. Here she developed her now world-famous teaching method. Possibly Montessori's most revolutionary belief was the importance of the child's environment when learning. She felt that for children to flourish and grow in self-esteem, they needed to work in a child-centered environment. Today, not only Montessori schools, but all schools recognize the part that the environment has to play in the development of the child.

Montessori always claimed that she did not devise a teaching method but that her ideas merely grew out of close observation of children. Montessori principles are based on the needs of the child, including the need to be independent, to find joy in learning, to enjoy order, to be respected and listened to, and to discover both fact and fiction. Today, these needs remain unchanged and are as relevant now as when they were first observed in 1909.

HOW TO USE THIS BOOK

This book is based on key Montessori principles of learning through experience, but rest assured, there is no need to create a Montessori classroom in your own home. The activities require little preparation and use readily available materials. You may be worried that you have no specialist knowledge of teaching; do not worry!

The points set out on the opposite page will guide you through the essential steps when presenting an activity to your child.

A NOTE ON HOW TO HANDLE SCISSORS WITH CHILDREN

Before learning to cut, children need to learn how to handle scissors safely. Teach your child that when carrying scissors, the scissors need to be held with the whole hand wrapped around the closed blades. Show her how to pass the scissors with the handle facing the person receiving them.

- To avoid repetition, the use of "she" and "he" is alternated in the activities. All the activities are suitable for boys and girls.

- Check your environment. Make sure that you and your child can do the activity in comfort and safety.

- Make sure that your child can see the activity clearly. Sit your child to the left of you (or to your right if she is left-handed).

- Aim to work with your right hand (or your left hand, if your child is left-handed) for consistency.

- Many of the activities are set on a tray. This defines the work space for your child. Choose a tray that is not patterned, to avoid distraction.

- Prepare the activity in advance. There is no point suggesting an activity to a child only to discover that you don't have the materials.

- Be orderly when presenting the activity. Set out your materials in an organized way and this will instill in your child a sense of order.

- Make your child responsible for carrying the materials to the work space and then returning them when the activity is completed. This creates a "cycle of work," and encourages your child to focus on the project.

- Be clear in your own mind of the aim of the activity, so always read through the exercise first.

- Do not interrupt when your child is working. Learn to sit back and observe.

- Try not to be negative. If your child is unable to do the activity correctly, then make a mental note to reintroduce it again at a later stage.

- If your child is absorbed by the activity and wishes to repeat it, let her do so, as many times as she wishes. A child learns through repetition.

- Create a work area for your child, if space permits. When an activity is over, leave the activity in a safe area, so your child can return to it if she wishes.

- If your child abuses any of the materials in the activity, then the activity needs to be removed immediately. By doing this, she will understand that her behavior was unacceptable. The activity can be reintroduced at a later date.

- Remember that at all times you are the role model and your child will model her behavior on your own.

FREQUENTLY ASKED QUESTIONS

How old should my child be before she is presented with an activity?

I have not set ages deliberately, as this can cause panic in parents if their child does not want to do a particular activity. Each child is an individual with different strengths and weaknesses and it is very rare to find a child who is confident in all areas of study. As a guideline, in a Montessori preschool, children are generally introduced to the activities in chapters one and two first, as these make a good foundation for the rest of the activities.

For children aged between four and five, I suggest that you introduce a selection of activities from all the chapters. The exception to this is if your child has a particular interest in a subject, for example, math, in which case you can present more of the numeracy activities.

Do I need to follow the order of the activities?

Aim to take each chapter in the order given, as it follows a natural progression. There is some flexibility, so you can try an activity, and then return to it at a later stage, if necessary. If your child is already confident in a skill, you might be able to introduce a later activity. However, it does not hurt to review knowledge, and this can increase a child's confidence.

If an activity is graded, when can my child progress to the next level of the activity?

In the boxes called "Also try," you will find progression activities that are ordered from easiest to hardest. Once your child has mastered one activity, and she feels confident to work independently, then present the next level of the activity.

What if my child is confused with the activity?

If your child demonstrates that she is confused with the activity, it is most likely that she is not ready for it. Consider also if your own modeling of the demonstration was done slowly and clearly enough and that you fully understood the purpose of the activity.

When is the best time in the day to present the activities?

Children, like adults, are more receptive during certain times of the day. The majority of children are at their most receptive in the morning, so more demanding activities should be done at this time. The other activities can be done at any time, but I would advise against doing them past mid-afternoon.

What if my child does not seem to respond to this activity?

If your child seems to be showing no interest in the activity, do not worry or get cross with your child. Simply put the activity away. Go through the presentation points alone. Ask yourself, did I present the activity in an appealing way? Was it the right time of the day? Did I understand my aim and did my child understand what was required? Consider whether your child was ready for that activity.

How do I use the worksheets?

When using the worksheets at the back of the book, photocopy them onto 11 x 17in. size paper, enlarging them to fit the full paper size. This way there will be plenty of space for your child to use each worksheet and they can be reused many times over.

DEVELOPING THE SENSES

Young children have heightened senses, and use them fully to expand their knowledge of the world. All the activities in this chapter not only help to stimulate and develop all five senses but also introduce new concepts and vocabulary.

As adults we tend to use mainly our senses of sight and hearing. When presenting these activities to your child, try to use all your senses, as your child will. In this way, you will begin to appreciate the value of these activities for your child's development.

SENSORY WALK

Everyone enjoys the sensation of walking on grass with bare feet, and for young children this pleasure is doubled because they have a heightened sense of touch. In this activity, a sensory trail of different textures is laid out for your child to explore and develop her sense of touch. It also has the advantage of developing balancing skills.

You will need

- Large indoor or outdoor space
- 4 cushions of any size (if possible, choose cushions with different fabrics)
- Carpet samples (from your local carpet store)
- Small rug
- Doormat (make sure it's not rough)
- Large sheet of bubble wrap

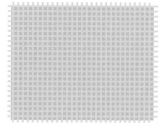

Activity

1 Lay a straight path with your chosen items, each of which should have a different texture.

2 Demonstrate to your child how you would like her to walk the path, with arms out to help her balance.

3 Let your child try it out.

4 She will need your support at first, so begin by holding each hand. When she is more confident with this activity, let her take a few steps by herself, but be close by in case you need to steady her again.

5 Walking over the cushions will be the trickiest part, so a steadying hand from you will be required for this.

Let your child repeat the path walk as many times as she wishes.

Also try

After your child has mastered the path, change the order of the surfaces and introduce some new ones.

Progress from a straight path to a wavy one.

SORT IT OUT

Young children love investigating a pile of objects and sorting them into groups. It satisfies their love of order and gives them a lot of information about the world around them.

You will need

- 4 to 6 different types of large buttons (large enough not to be a choking hazard)
- Enough small containers for each type of button

Remember that buttons can be a choking hazard, so choose ones as large as possible and supervise your child during this activity.

Activity

1 Put a container with all the buttons combined together in the center.

2 Place all the other containers around it in a circle.

3 Ask your child if he thinks all the buttons are the same color and shape.

4 Tell him that he is going to sort them out into the separate containers.

5 Start by putting a button of each type into each container so that it is clear which button needs to go where.

6 Ask your child to sort through the buttons and put them into the correct containers.

7 Once all the buttons have been sorted, he may want to do the activity again.

Also try

Don't just stop at buttons. Plenty of other objects can be used for sorting, such as small pieces of fabric, toy cars, and toy animals.

DISTINGUISHING SOUNDS

This activity shows your child that when an object is struck, it emits a sound. She will then be asked to consider the quality of the sound and whether it is "loud" or "soft." When she has mastered this skill, try to refine these listening skills by grading each sound from loudest to softest. As with all the activities in this chapter, along with the understanding of the concept comes the language to describe it.

You will need

- 4 to 6 objects that make a loud or soft sound, such as two saucepan lids banged together or a jar of coffee to shake
- Large tray to carry the objects

Activity

1   Ask your child to sit where she can see clearly and place the tray in front of you.

2   Tell your child, "We are going to listen to the sounds these objects make and describe whether it is a loud or soft sound."

3   Select an object that you know has a loud sound. Make its sound and then say the word "loud" and place it on the left. Repeat with an object with a soft sound and place it on the right.

4   Pass over the objects and invite your child to sort the rest of the sounds into soft sounds and loud sounds.

Safety point: After this activity, discuss with your child the dangers of making loud sounds very close to the ears, and how this can damage the hearing.

GUESS THE SOUND GAME

Try this experiment: Stop and count how many different sounds you hear in one day. I think you will be very surprised at the total. Many of these sounds you will have blanked out, for your brain has understood and recognized them. But for a child the majority of these sounds will be unknowns that need to be identified. This fun game will help children in building up their knowledge of different sounds, while the later activities will encourage them to identify these sounds and refine their hearing abilities.

You will need

- Large tray
- Cloth large enough to cover the tray
- A selecton of objects that make interesting sounds. Don't use musical instruments as they could distract from the game

Remind your child that making a loud sound close to the ears can damage the hearing. If your child has any difficulty with this activity, have his hearing checked.

Activity

1 Ask your child to sit on your left with the tray in front of you. Place the objects on the tray.

2 Tell your child, "We are going to play guess the sound." Point to and name aloud all of the objects on the tray.

3 Cover the tray with the cloth. Select an object under the cloth, for example, the two spoons. Knock these together, asking your child to listen to the sound.

Also try

As your child becomes more confident, add extra objects, to a maximum of six, and start to introduce new objects with unfamiliar sounds.

As he grows older and more familiar with the objects and their names, ask him to try and guess which object he thinks made that noise.

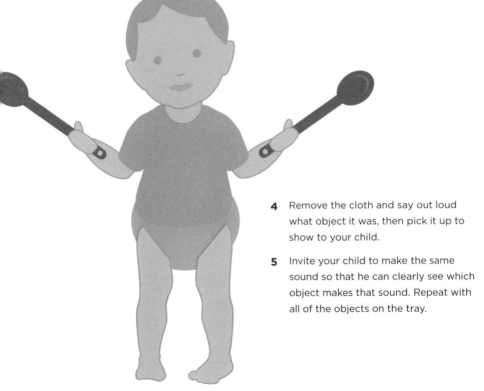

4 Remove the cloth and say out loud what object it was, then pick it up to show to your child.

5 Invite your child to make the same sound so that he can clearly see which object makes that sound. Repeat with all of the objects on the tray.

COMPARING SOUNDS

Your child has learned how to compare different levels of sounds
and to grade them from the loudest to the softest. Here, listening skills
are further refined as your child is required to match up sounds. This might
sound easy, but requires careful listening and concentration. There are no
visual aids and she must rely entirely on memory of the sound until
she listens to the next one.

You will need

- 6 small cylinder-shaped opaque lidded containers
- Assorted dried lentils, beans, peas, and rice
- 2 containers or baskets

Half-fill two of the lidded containers with lentils. Repeat with two other dried foods. Divide the pairs and put three of each in one container or basket and the other three in the other container.

Also try

Increase the number of canisters until your child is matching up to six pairs of sounds. You could use sugar, coffee, and breakfast cereal in the canisters for new sounds.

Activity

1. Ask your child to carry one container or basket, while you carry the other to the table.

2. Invite your child to sit on your left. Put one container on your left and the other on your right toward the back of the table. Take the canisters out of the containers and place them in front of you.

3. Say to your child, "I am going to match and pair up the different sounds." Pick up a canister from the left side, with your right hand, and shake it to listen.

4. Pick up a canister from the right side, with your right hand, and shake it to listen.

5. Go back to the first canister to check if it matches the sound. Keep trying the canisters on the right side until you find the matching sound. When you do, pair the canisters and put them in front of you starting at the left. Continue until all the canisters are matched.

6. Invite your child to match and pair the sounds. Set out the canisters, ready for your child to try the activity. Afterward, you might like to open the canisters to check that she was right.

IDENTIFYING TASTES

In this activity, your child will discover that while every food has its own flavor, it also has an overriding quality of sweetness, sourness, or saltiness. He will sort the food into three sets, and in order to isolate the taste, the activity is done blindfolded. You may think that your child will be unwilling to try foods blindfolded, but I have found that once a child sees an adult doing this, they are reassured.

You will need

- 3 foods, one each that is sweet, sour, or salty, such as apple slices, lemon slices, and salted chips
- 3 small dishes
- Paper towels
- Tray
- Eye mask

Prepare the food into slices or bite-size pieces. Put each food onto one of the dishes and place on the tray. Place the paper towels alongside them on the tray.

Activity

1   Ask your child to sit where they can see clearly and have the tray in front of you with the paper towel closest to you. For this activity, the work area will be on the tray.

2   Tell him, "I am going to taste the food and see if it tastes salty, sour, or sweet, but I only want to taste with my tongue, and not look with my eyes."

3   Put on the eye mask. Select a food; if it tastes salty, it goes on the paper on the left of the tray. The sour food goes in the middle, and the sweet on the right. As you are tasting each food, say,

"This tastes salty [or sour or sweet]." Continue until all the foods have been tasted.

4   Remove the eye mask and invite your child to sort the food. If there are some foods that he is not familiar with or is reluctant to try, suggest that he licks the food or takes a "baby" bite to taste them. If he is very keen on the food, allow him to eat it, and then ask him to take another piece to put on the paper.

Also try

Change some of the foods and increase the number of foods tasted from three to five or eight.

GUESS THE FRUIT OR VEGETABLE

This activity is designed to help your child develop her sense of touch by exploring the shape and textures of different fruit and vegetables. At the same time she will extend her knowledge of fruit and vegetables.

You will need

- 3 fruits or vegetables, all different in size, shape, and texture; for example, an apple, a banana, a potato
- Eye mask or blindfold

If your child is having difficulty identifying the fruit or vegetable say the names out loud. This should help, but give her plenty of time before stepping in. Remember that this is a sensory activity so don't overburden your child with too much language.

Activity

1   Explain to your child that you are going to play guess the fruit or vegetable.

2   Ask her to help carry the fruit and vegetables to the activity area. This could be the floor or a low table.

3   Place the fruit and vegetables in the center of the activity area, along with the eye mask.

4   Go through with your child the names of the fruit or vegetables you are using.

5   Demonstrate how to put on the eye mask.

6   Reach out to choose a fruit or vegetable. Take time to feel it, while commenting on its shape, size, and texture.

7   Guess the name of the fruit or vegetable and say it out loud.

8   Remove the eye mask and pass it to your child for her to try. Some children may get upset by the eye mask, in which case simply ask her to close her eyes or cover them with her hands instead.

GUESS THE FOOD

Food forms a major part of any child's life and as children are growing up it is important that they develop a positive attitude toward it. This activity invites your child to explore and test his knowledge of foods through taste alone. It can also be a good opportunity to introduce him to new foods once he has mastered the game; as he watches you trying the new food it will encourage him to try it as well.

You will need

- 6 distinctively flavored foods
- 6 small plates or containers
- Eye mask or blindfold
- Tray

Activity

1 Put each food on a separate plate or container and place in a row on the tray along with the mask. Put the tray on the table.

2 Invite your child to sit next to you and say, "Let us play guess the food."

3 Start by asking him to taste each food and say its name one at a time.

4 Demonstrate by putting on the mask or blindfold and sampling one of the foods, then saying its name, for example: "I think this is the baked bean."

5 Take off the mask or blindfold and invite him to try.

6 Ask him to put on the mask or blindfold and guide his hand to one of the plates. Let him try the food and if he guesses correctly, move the plate to the right. For those he gets wrong, put the plate to the left to try again later.

CONTRASTING SMELLS

Children will always comment on what they think of the smells around them, so your child will enjoy this activity. It requires her to sort various smells into pleasant and unpleasant ones. You will also give your child the opportunity to increase her vocabulary to describe different smells. While you want your child to explore the smells around her, make her aware that certain substances give off fumes. Toxic household products should not be used for this project and should be locked away safely at all times.

You will need

- 6 items with contrasting smells, such as perfume, aftershave, aromatherapy oils, flowers, citrus fruits, coffee, and vinegar (don't use household cleaning products, as they can be harmful when inhaled)
- 6 small containers, such as jars with lids
- Cotton pads or balls
- Tray

Activity

1 Soak each cotton pad or ball with a different smell. If you are using a citrus fruit, squeeze over some of its juice. The reason for this is to isolate the smell from the food. Put each cotton pad in a separate container and put the lid on, or cover with plastic wrap or aluminum foil.

2 Leave the containers for about five minutes so that the smell infuses the cotton pad.

3 Select one jar with a nice smell and put it on the front right-hand corner of the tray and then select a jar with a nasty smell and put it on the front left-hand corner. Put the rest of the jars at the back of the tray.

4 Ask your child to sit where she can see clearly, and put the tray in front of you in the middle. Tell your child that you are going to sort the smells into nice and nasty smells.

5 Pick up the jar on the right-hand side with the pleasant smell, open it, smell it, and say, "That's a very nice smell," and then put it on the right-hand side of the table. Show your child that you are taking your time smelling before deciding what kind of smell it is.

Also try

Increase the number of smells from six to eight.

Play a game matching smells, using two sets of containers, each containing matching pairs of smells. Place one of each at either end of a tray and show your child how to look for a matching smell.

6 Repeat with the jar with the nasty smell and say something like, "I don't like that smell; it's nasty." Put the jar on the left-hand side of the table.

7 Invite your child to finish sorting the smells so that she finishes with the nasty smells on the left and the nice smells on the right.

8 Set up the jars in exactly the same way in front of your child for her to try the whole activity.

GUESS THE SMELL

Smell is one of our most potent senses; it is amazing how a smell can hold and release a memory such as a vacation or a place. In this simple but effective game, your child will have the opportunity to distinguish different smells and then test her memory of them.

You will need

- 6 liquid or ground items with contrasting smells (see tip)
- Cotton pads or balls
- 6 small containers with lids
- Small tray

Activity

1   Put each of your chosen scented items on a cotton ball or pad. Place each in a container and close the lid.

2   Put the containers in a row on a tray and then place on a table.

3   Invite your child to sit next to you and say to her, "Let us play guess the smell." Remind your child how well they did with the contrasting smells game.

Aromatherapy oils are very good for choosing contrasting smells, for example, lavender, tea tree, or citrus juice. Herbs are another good option.

You may wish to start with three containers, and then work up to six.

Choose smells with which she is familiar.

Your child may wish to close her eyes as this helps to focus on the smell.

Also try

This is a good opportunity to explain to your child that some substances could be harmful if smelled, so they should always check with an adult.

As a child I loved trying to make perfume from rose petals. You could set up a perfume store role-play game.

Collect assorted jars and bottles and help your child to make labels for the perfume bottles. She could also make a perfume store label.

4   Start by showing her all the scents; one at a time, ask her to open up each container. Smell it yourself and say the name of the smell. Pass it to her, ask her to smell and then repeat the name.

5   Next, tell her that this time she must smell each container herself and try to tell you the smell.

6   When your child smells each scent again, ask her to put the containers for those she is sure of to the right and those she is unsure of to the left, to try again later.

FOLLOWING A TRAIL

Children love following a trail, especially if they know there's going to be treasure at the end. This game can be played with as many or as few children as you wish. It's also a great game for older siblings to join in. For those reluctant walkers, they will be so busy having fun following the trail they won't even realize all the exercise they're getting.

You will need

- Outdoor space
- Piece of chalk
- Small bag of flour
- Treasure (such as stickers, cookies, chocolate coins)

Activity

1 Choose your outdoor space. You could use a large garden, park, or woodland— whatever is available or nearby.

2 Set a trail using the chalk to mark the way with large arrows, or blobs of flour when there isn't a place for an arrow.

3 Your trail should take about 30 minutes of walking time.

4 Explain to the children that they are going to follow a trail and that they need to look out for white arrows and blobs of flour.

When following the trail, don't let the children race too far ahead of you. Always keep them within your sight.

5   Ask one child to choose three of his favorite movements and have the others copy his sequence.

6   When they get to the end of the trail, reward them with their treasure. This could be anything from a special sticker to their favorite cookie or you could even hide some chocolate coins.

Make sure all your chalk arrows and blobs of flour are clearly visible at a child's sight level.

LEARNING HEIGHT AND LENGTH

Using rods to introduce the concept of length, your child will build a stair of rods from the shortest to the longest. He will be required to estimate the length of each rod and where it fits into the stair. You can discuss the same concept by showing photographs of family members, and their varying heights; you could even get everyone to line up in a row, from tallest to shortest!

You will need

- Worksheet 1
- Sheet of tabloid size paper
- Large sheet of thick cardboard
- Scissors
- Blue and red markers
- Glue
- Tray

Photocopy and enlarge the worksheet onto paper. Color in the sections blue and red, starting with red for the single section, then blue for the longest section. The first rod will have one section, the second, two (one of each color), the third, three sections, and so on. Cut out the rods and stick them onto the card. Then cut them out, as shown.

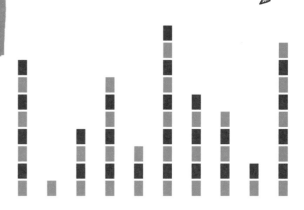

Activity

1 Arrange the rods in a random order on a tray, so he can see them clearly.

2 Put the rods horizontally in front of you and make sure he can watch.

3 Tell him that you are going to build the rods into a staircase starting with the shortest.

4 Select the shortest rod and put it in front of you. When you are selecting your rod, run your right hand along to the end so that he will see that you are finding the next length.

5 Build up the rest of the staircase finishing with the longest rod.

6 Tell him that you are going to dismantle the staircase so that he can build it.

7 Take the rods one at a time and place them to the right of him in a random order.

8 Invite him to build the staircase.

Make sure the ends of the colored rods on the left-hand side are lined up straight, so that your child will clearly see the stair effect.

Also try

Take every opportunity to reinforce the mathematical language of long and short. You could ask your child to compare the height of members of the family. Ask, "Who is the shortest?" and, "Who is the tallest?"

You could also introduce the mathematical language of weight: "heavy" and "light." Ask him to compare the different weights of food items by using his hands as scales.

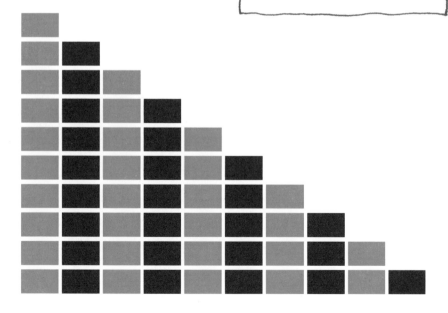

DISCOVERING COLORS

Children are drawn to color. These color activities begin by matching the primary colors, then secondary colors, and finally grading shades of one color. They use the paint color sample strips that you can find in hardware stores. Choose the brightest primary colors that you can find.

You will need

- 6 paint color sample strips (2 each of red, blue, and yellow)
- Scissors
- Container or basket

Select and cut out the rectangles that are the brightest shade on the color strips so that you have two matching reds, two matching blues, and two matching yellows. Put the colored rectangles in the container.

Activity

1   Ask your child to carry the container to the table and to sit where she can see clearly.

2   With the container in front of you, remove all the rectangles. Put half the pieces in a row horizontally, and the other half below in a vertical column.

3   Say to her that you are going to match up the colors. Starting with the bottom color in the vertical row, find the matching color from the horizontal row and pair them up.

4   Invite her to finish the matching.

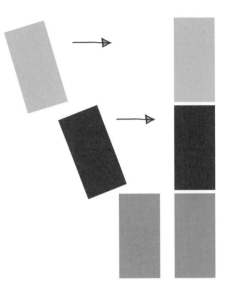

Also try

Add more rectangles using the secondary colors of green, orange, and purple.

Progress to matching shades of one color. Cut rectangles from the color strips of the same color shade. Invite her to match up all the shades of the one color. See also the activity on the next page.

DISCOVERING COLORS 2

Once your child has learned about the primary and secondary colors, you can move on to different shades of color. He will be required to match the color cards in terms of shading difference. As an extension activity, you could then ask him to arrange from lightest to darkest.

You will need

- **2 matching paint swatches, any color**
- **Scissors**

Activity

1   Cut up one of the paint swatches into the individual shades.

2   Place these in a small pile with the uncut swatch just above it.

3   Invite your child to join you and explain that you would like to show him something about color.

4   Ask him to spread out the cut pieces and explain that he needs to match up the colors.

5   Demonstrate to him by matching up one or two pieces.

6   Let him continue and complete the activity.

Also try

Using the cut pieces, ask your child to arrange the colors from lightest to darkest, from top to bottom. He should find the lightest first, then the darkest, and then the other colors between.

You may not wish to use all the shades to start with; instead use four, and then work up to the complete set.

When demonstrating, go slowly and really exaggerate searching for the matching color shade so your child understands what is needed.

EXPLORING TEMPERATURES

This activity uses your child's sense of touch to sort materials by temperature from the coldest to the hottest. It is an excellent introduction to many topics, including why certain materials are best for certain types of jobs and how the body has a higher temperature when we are unwell.

You will need

- 3 to 8 materials of contrasting temperature (for example, metal, ceramic tile, wood or cork, marble, yarn, plastic)
- Tray, preferably plain
- Eye mask or blindfold (optional)

Choosing a surface

Choose contrasting materials, such as fabric, metal, ceramic tile, wood or cork, marble, yarn, plastic.

Activity

1 Start by placing all the materials in a row on a tray along with the mask or blindfold.

2 Invite your child to the table and show her the collection of materials. Tell her that the materials need to be sorted by temperature from the coldest to the hottest or warmest.

3 Put on the mask or blindfold and explain that you are now "looking" for the coldest piece of material. Feel each piece of material in turn until the coldest piece is found. Select it and place on the bottom left-hand side of the table.

4 Repeat this step to find the hottest piece and place it on the right-hand side with space between. Repeat this step with the other materials until they have all been selected.

5 Take off the mask or blindfold and put the materials back onto the tray. Invite your child to do the activity.

6 After she has put on the mask, guide her hand toward the tray and remind her that she is first searching for the coldest material and then the hottest, and so on.

Also try

Think of other opportunities to talk about temperatures, for example, the weather, cooking, refrigerator thermometers, bath water, food such as hot chocolate or ice cream, how ice is made.

For younger children, start with just three or four materials and then add more.

The mask heightens the sense of touch, but it is optional as some children feel uncomfortable with it. If this is the case, instead ask them to close their eyes.

INTRODUCING TEXTURAL OPPOSITES

This very simple activity introduces the terms "rough" and "smooth," using graded sandpaper. Sandpaper is an excellent material for stimulating tactile awareness and for illustrating the textural opposites of rough and smooth. Before starting, your child will need to wash his hands in order to sensitize his fingers.

You will need

- Sheet of rough sandpaper
- Sheet of smooth sandpaper
- Container or basket

Activity

1 Cut each sheet of sandpaper into about six pieces and place them in the container or basket.

2 Ask your child to sit where he can see clearly and put the basket in front of you. Take out the sandpaper pieces and put them in a row in front of the basket.

3 Say to him, "I am going to feel the sandpaper and find out if it is rough or smooth."

4 Beginning at the left, feel across the row of pieces using the fingertips of your second and third fingers only. When you find a rough piece, say the word "rough." Place this on your left.

5 Return to the row and feel to find a piece of smooth sandpaper. When found, say the word "smooth." Put the smooth piece of sandpaper on your right.

6   Pass the two pieces over to him and invite him to stroke his fingertips over them in the same way. When he has felt the surfaces, get him to feel them again, but this time say the words "rough" and "smooth" and get him to repeat them.

7   Now pick up the sandpaper pieces and put them in front of you. Sort the rest of the pieces into rough and smooth piles of sandpaper. Say the words "rough" or "smooth" as you feel each piece.

8   Put all the sandpaper in a random order back in the container and invite him to sort the sandpaper.

Always work from left to right, even if your child is left-handed. This is to prepare him for reading.

Also try

Introduce two other grades of sandpaper—for example, very rough and very smooth. Repeat the activity, but say, "I am going to feel which is the roughest piece." When found, say, "This is the roughest piece of sandpaper," and place it to one side. Repeat the action, feeling which is the smoothest piece. When you have found it, put it on the right side.

LEARNING TACTILE OPPOSITES

Your child will need to consider the substance of an object and how this affects the tactile experience. Once this concept is understood, then she will have learned that objects that yield to the touch are "soft," and objects that resist are "hard." Like the previous activities, you start by introducing opposites, and once this is learned, you expand upon this, so it is very important that you follow the steps in order.

You will need

- 6 to 8 small objects that are hard or soft, such as marbles, wood, playdough
- Container or basket

Activity

1 With the basket in front of you and your child sitting where she can see, take out a hard object from the basket. Put it on your left. Take out a soft object and put it on your right.

2 Press your fingertips into the hard object and say the word "hard." Repeat the action with the soft object and say the word "soft."

3 Pass the two objects over to your child, and invite her to feel the surfaces, as you did.

4 When she has felt the surfaces, get her to feel them again, but this time say the words "hard" and "soft."

5 Invite your child to sort the rest of the objects into hard or soft.

Choose contrasting objects so your child can clearly feel the difference between hard and soft. Really press your fingers into the object so that your child understands that soft objects yield to the touch.

Also try

Show your child how to grade objects from hardest to softest.

Introduce a blindfold so your child grades the objects through touch alone. When showing your child how to do it, say, "I am feeling for the hardest object," and place it to your left. Then say, "I am feeling for the softest object," and continue, comparing with the other objects in the row until you have graded all the objects.

Show your child how to sort objects by temperature (coldest and warmest). Choose objects with contrasting temperatures, such as cork, marble, wood, stone, and yarn. Try the temperature activity using an eye mask. See activity on page 42.

COMPARING TEXTURES

Playing with fabrics teaches your child to sort, grade, and match. The sandpaper activities need to be completed before attempting this because your child will need to have learned the terms "rough," "smooth," "roughest," and "smoothest." This activity uses an eye mask, to encourage your child to sort the fabric by "feel." You will need to read all the steps before you start!

You will need

- 6 pieces of fabric
  4 x 4 in. (10 x 10 cm)
- Container
- Eye mask or blindfold

Choosing fabrics

Choose contrasting fabrics, such as silk, satin, cotton, cord, velvet, wool, and burlap.

If you ask your child a question, be sure to give her clues or pointers to help her answer rather than volunteering the answer. Give her plenty of time to think about it.

Also try

Take every opportunity to find surfaces that are rough or smooth, and encourage your child to feel them. For example, say to your child, "I wonder if the bark of that tree is rough or smooth," or "I wonder if that leaf is rough or smooth," or "I wonder which is smoother or rougher, the leaf or the bark?"

Activity

1   Arrange the pieces of fabric in a row in front of the basket. Say to your child, "I am going to feel which fabrics are rough and which are smooth, but to make sure I only use my fingers to feel, I am going to cover my eyes." Put on the eye mask.

2   Feel across the row and select a rough piece of fabric. Feel the fabric, holding it between the thumb and second and third fingers, and make a rubbing action. Feel it again and say "rough." Place it to the left side of the table.

3   Feel the fabrics until you find a smooth fabric, say "smooth" and place it to the right side. Continue until all the fabrics have been sorted into two piles of rough and smooth.

4   Take off the eye mask and put it in the basket. Mix up the fabric pieces, then invite your child to try the activity. You might need to help her put on the eye mask. (Some children can be nervous about putting on an eye mask; if so, ask her to close her eyes instead.)

BE YOUR OWN SCALES

If asked to compare two objects by weight, most young children would say the bigger of the two objects was heaviest. This activity teaches your child that the weight of an object is not related to its size. It acts as a starting point for understanding that the weight of an object is measured by its mass. But we are going to start simply by asking your child to become a human scale and compare two contrasting objects. This will become more challenging when the objects become similar in shape and size.

You will need

- Set A) a variety of contrasting objects like a stone and a feather or a can of beans and a box of tea bags
- Set B) pairs more similar in size and weight

Activity

1 Show your child a set of weighing scales and ask him what he thinks they might be used for. If he is unsure, give him a demonstration of how to use them. Ask him why it might be useful to know the weight of something.

2 Explain to him that he is going to be like the scales and that his is going to compare two objects and guess which he thinks is heavier.

3 Chose two contrasting objects from set A and place one in each hand.

4 Demonstrate the comparison of the weight of the two objects by making a seesaw action.

5 Now ask him first what he thinks will be the heavier of the two objects before putting them into his hands.

6 Once he has understood the activity, move onto comparing the weight of the objects in set B.

Also try

When you are both out, ask your child to think about where he might find devices for weighing, for example, at the doctor's office, the airport for suitcases, when buying food.

When cooking together, get your child to help weigh out the ingredients.

Try the "Make your own balancing scales" activity on the following page.

MAKE YOUR OWN
BALANCING SCALES

This activity is a natural extension to the comparing weights activity where the same seesaw motion is used to compare the weights. A seesaw is a very good place to start to explain how a balance scale works. So it's a good idea to take a trip with your child to the local playground where hopefully there will be a seesaw. When there, ask her what would happen if there was a child at one end of the seesaw and an adult on the other, which end would go up and which would go down.

You will need

- A coat hanger that has 2 skirt hooks
- 4 pieces of wire of exactly the same width, around 14 in. (35 cm)
- 2 paper cups or clean yogurt containers
- Some small, light objects to be weighed, such as clothespins

Activity

1 Explain to your child that she is going to make a balance scale that will work in a similar way to the seesaw that she saw in the playground.

2 Wrap one piece of wire around the outer rim of one of the cups leaving an 8 in. (20 cm) length left over.

3 Repeat the same steps with another piece of wire. Join the two 8 in. (20 cm) lengths by twisting the wire together. This will form the hanging handle of one of your balances.

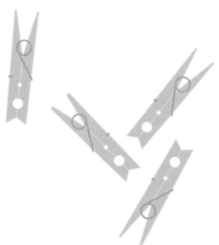

4 Repeat the same steps with the
   other cup.

5 Carefully hang each cup by the wire
   handle in the center on each coat
   hanger hook.

6 Hang your completed balance over
   a door handle. The balance is now
   complete and your child can have fun
   weighing the different objects.

A piece of adhesive
putty or tape might
be needed to hold the
wire twists together.

Also try

If there is a marked difference in
weight between two objects, you
could explore how many more
of that object you would need to
make the scales balance.

Suggest to your child that she
think about what the objects are
made of and whether that could
be a factor in determining the
weight of the chosen object.

THE FEELY BAG GAME

Your child will really enjoy this game, which challenges his memory of touch, pulling together all the tactile experiences that he will have encountered in the previous activities. The aim of the game is to guess, by feeling, which of the selected objects have been put in the bag. It can also teach new vocabulary, as you can ask him how he guessed the object in the bag.

You will need

- 3 to 5 different objects, such as a couple of favorite toys, an apple, etc.
- Drawstring bag
- Container or basket
- Small towel

Choose contrasting objects, with different shapes and textures, and include some favorite objects, such as toys.

For younger children, start off with just three objects, and work up to five.

Activity

1   Show your child the objects you have in your container or basket one at a time, and name them.

2   Explain to your child that he is going to have to guess which object you have put into the bag, just by feeling it. Ask your child to turn away and to shut his eyes.

3   Select an object and put it in the bag. Cover up the other objects with the towel.

4   Ask your child to open his eyes and pass him the bag. Ask him if he can guess the object in the bag. Give him time to explore the object and if he doesn't seem sure, you could remind him of the objects—for example, "Do you think it is the ball?"

Also try

As your child gains confidence in this activity, put two objects, then three, into the bag at the same time.

5   When he has guessed correctly, choose another object and continue until all the objects have been guessed.

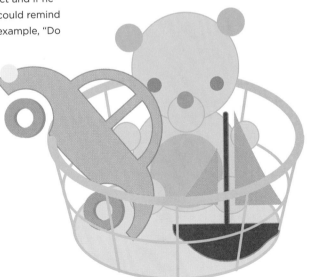

MATCHING 2D SHAPES

This activity concentrates on the mathematical concept of shape. Your child will learn how to identify a circle and how to estimate the difference between the sizes of the circles. The cutout circles are matched up to ones drawn on paper. This acts as a control so that your child will be able to see if she has estimated correctly, and to make corrections herself. In the "Also try," the same activity is repeated with squares and triangles.

You will need

- **Worksheet 2**
- **Sheets of 8.5 x 11 in. paper**
- **Scissors**
- **Container or basket**

Always work from left to right, even if your child is left-handed. This is to prepare her for reading. Take time when choosing your circles, looking back and forth from the sheet to the paper circles. In this way, your child will see that you are comparing sizes.

Activity

1   Photocopy the worksheet a few times onto stiff paper. Cut out one set of circles and place in the container or basket. Leave at least one sheet intact.

2   Ask your child to carry the container to the table, while you carry the worksheet. Ask your child to sit where she can see clearly. Put the worksheet in front of you and put the container behind it.

3   Take out the circles and place in a random order in a row behind the worksheet.

4   Tell your child that you are going to match the circles, starting with the biggest and ending with the smallest.

5   Select the biggest paper circle and match it up to the circle on the sheet. Continue until all the circles are matched up.

6   Put the circles back into the container and pass it, along with the worksheet, to your child to try.

Also try

On Worksheet 2 you will see two other sections, one with squares and one with triangles. Repeat the activity by matching the squares and then the triangles.

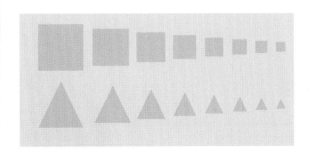

MATCHING 3D SHAPES

This activity progresses from the last, in that the shapes now reappear in 3D (three dimensions). The shapes used are familiar objects, which are then given their correct mathematical names and sorted into pairs. Using familiar objects will help your child to memorize the mathematical names.

You will need

- 2 spheres, such as tennis balls or marbles
- 2 cubes, such as building blocks
- 2 cylinders, such as small cans
- Container or basket

Activity

1   Ask your child to carry the container to the table and place it in front of her in the middle. Tell your child that she is going to match up the solid shapes.

2   Say to your child, "Can you find me a building block which is a cube shape?" When she has selected the block, ask her to place it on the left.

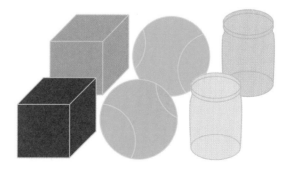

3   Ask the same question, but ask for a sphere and then a cylinder.

4   Ask your child to pair up the solid shapes left in the box with those on the table.

5   Increase the number of solids gradually until your child can match six pairs.

Also try

You could include other three-dimensional shapes, such as cones, pyramids, and ovoids. You might have toys these shapes, but you could use an ice-cream cone and a hard-boiled egg, and show a photograph of a pyramid.

You can play "The feely bag game" from the following page. Use one sphere, cylinder, and cube. Show each to your child, one at a time, saying its name. Ask your child to close her eyes, while you put one of the solids in the bag. Hide the other two solids and ask your child to open her eyes. Pass the bag to her to feel the solid and to try and guess which one it is.

MATCHING 3D SHAPES WITH FEELY BAG

Here is a natural progression from two-dimensional to three-dimensional shapes that also reinforces the names of the 3D shapes to your child. Using the feely bag reminds children that we can use our sense of touch as well as our vision when identifying objects.

You will need

- **3 3D shapes (cylinder, sphere, and cube)**
- **Drawstring bag**

Activity

1   Place the three shapes in a row on a table along with the drawstring bag.

2   Invite your child to the table and remind her how well she did with the 3D shape matching game. Explain that this is a fun activity to help learn the names of the shapes in front of her.

3   To introduce the names of the three shapes, pick one shape up, feel it while saying the name, and then pass it to her to do the same. Repeat for the other two shapes.

4   Now touch each shape in turn, say the name, and ask her to repeat it.

5   Say to her, "Show me the cylinder," and ask her to point to it. Do the same for the other shapes.

6   Ask her to close her eyes and then put one of the shapes into the feely bag. Ask her to put her hand into the bag and see if she is able to guess the shape. Repeat with the other shapes.

For younger children, start with just two shapes.

If your child is still not confident with the names after this activity, reintroduce it.

Also try

When your child is confident with this activity, you could introduce the written names of the shapes. Write out the names of the shapes on separate pieces of card. Introduce the names using the same steps as opposite. When she is confident with the written names, ask her to match the shapes with the written names.

MUSICAL SCALES

Here, the harmonics of sound are introduced by making a musical scale from bottles filled with different levels of water. Your child will also be introduced to high and low sounds and the idea that harmonics of sound only work in a certain order. Explain to your child the dangers of broken glass. Let him see you handling and carrying with care and he will learn to do the same.

You will need

- 5 glass bottles or glasses
- Water
- Teaspoon
- Food coloring (optional)

Color the water first to add interest to the activity. Fill the bottles or glasses with different levels of water to make a scale of sounds. Tap each with the teaspoon to check for a contrasting sound. If you need to make more of a contrast between the sounds, adjust the amount of water in the bottles.

Activity

1   Show your child how to carry each bottle or glass, one by one, safely to the table, with one hand on the base and one on the side.

2   With your child on your left, put the bottles in front of you in a row, toward the back of the table.

3   Say to him, "I am going to show you how to make a musical scale. First, I need to listen to find the lowest sound." Pick up the spoon and gently tap the sides of the bottles or glasses to find the lowest sound. When you have found the right bottle, take it out of the row and put it on the left.

4   Say to him, "Now I need to listen to find the highest sound." Repeat the action and select the highest sound and put the bottle on the right, leaving a space for the other three bottles.

5   Invite your child to complete the scale, saying, "I have found the bottle with the lowest sound [tap the bottle] and the one with the highest sound [tap the bottle]. Now can you order the sounds that come in between." Set the bottles up in front of your child so that he can complete the scale.

Also try

From making a scale using five bottles, progress to eight, which is the number in a full musical scale.

If your child comments on the different bottle sizes or the water in them making a difference in the pitch of the sounds, let your child experiment with these ideas.

EXPLORING THE MAGICAL PROPERTIES OF CORNSTARCH

This activity is an excellent introduction for children learning about liquids and solids. The cornstarch is "magical" because it can behave one moment like a liquid and the next like a solid (with some quick stirring). Your child will have fun exploring cornstarch's magical properties.

You will need

- **Large mixing bowl**
- **Cornstarch**
- **Pitcher of water**
- **Wooden spoon**
- **Tray or wipe-clean tablecloth**
- **Apron**
- **Food coloring (optional)**

Activity

1. Place the bowl along with the cornstarch, water, food coloring, and spoon onto the tray or covered table.

2. Invite your child over and explain to him that you would like to show him this special flour and the challenge is to try and make it into a ball by adding the water. Put an apron on him.

3. Ask him to spoon out some flour into the bowl and then add a little water with about 4 drops of food coloring (if used).

4. Ask him to stir the flour and water and observe what happens.

5. Ask him if it makes a difference if he changes the speed of his stirring.

6. When the mix gets to the right consistency (see tip), he should be able to make a ball; ask him if he is able to roll the ball or if it changes back into a liquid.

The ratio needed is roughly 2:1 cornstarch to water, so advise your child to add the water slowly. If the cornstarch does not form into a ball, then more cornstarch is needed.

Also try

You could use your cornstarch slime for various small-world and role-play activities, for example, pour onto a baking sheet and add toy dinosaurs.

Create a science lab with white coats, safety goggles, jars of colored water, and, of course, your cornstarch slime.

THE WACKY RACES

All toddlers with toy cars enjoy racing them across every surface in the house. It's their way of discovering different textures. Taking my inspiration from this, the next activity recreates a miniature multisurface racetrack using whatever materials you have to hand. Avoid materials that could be a potential choking or blocked nasal hazard.

You will need

- Large tray or baking sheet
- Aluminum foil to line the tray
- Marker
- Medium-size ball of playdough or plasticine
- Selection of materials for the racetrack, all with different textures. Here are some possible materials you may like to use (you can of course try some of your own): crushed eggshells, egg cartons, sand, shells, corrugated cardboard, marbles, buttons, pieces of bark, twigs
- Toy cars

Activity

1 Line the tray with the aluminum foil.

2 With the marker, mark out a winding wacky racetrack with lots of hairpin bends.

3 Take the playdough and roll it into long thin "snakes." If he is able, invite your child to help you with this.

4 Line the snakes on the foil so they follow the line of the marked racetrack. This will act as a barrier and contain the material.

5 Choose a material and fill in a section of racetrack. The area each material covers will depend upon how many materials you have. For the activity to be really effective, you should have as many materials as possible. I would suggest a minimum of four.

6 Continue sectioning the racetrack until it is complete. It is now ready for racing.

7 Give your child a collection of toy cars and let him run them around the racetrack, so that he can feel the differences between all the surfaces that you have laid on the track.

Also try

You may wish to upgrade your racetrack with some of these suggestions:

Take small twigs with pine needles or leaves on them and stick them into the playdough to line the racetrack with trees.

You could make road signs with pieces of paper and popsicle sticks and again stick them into the playdough.

COORDINATION

We take for granted the ability to move our bodies. The degree of complexity of coordination involved in playing sports or the fine motor skills of using a keyboard or threading a needle in some ways define who we are. I have observed that children derive as much pleasure from mastering new physical skills as any language achievement. Control of their bodies gives them a sense of empowerment and self-confidence. In the following chapter you will find activities that will introduce and develop the gross and fine motor skills.

WHERE DOES IT GO?

Hand–eye coordination can be built up from the earliest stages with games that involve the simplest puzzling tasks, starting with fitting squares together and moving toward making a picture from the separate pieces. This activity shows you how to create materials for the most basic 3D puzzle, which can be developed as your child's skills improve.

You will need

- Collection of different-shaped objects or building blocks, such as a triangle, a square, and a circle
- Cardboard box
- Scissors or craft knife
- Adhesive tape

If she is having difficulty, try using the color of the shapes as a clue. Say, "It is one of the blue shapes," for example.

Activity

1   Gather together a number of different-shaped building blocks, such as a triangle, a square, and a circle.

2   Cut holes in the top of the cardboard box that are the same shape as the blocks you have chosen, but make the holes slightly larger. Tape up any open flaps so that there is no other way in except through the holes.

3   Give the first shape to your child. Guide her fingers around the edges, so that she traces the outline of the shape, and then do the same around the hole in the box so that she becomes familiar with the feel of the shape.

4 Ask her to put the shape through the matching hole. If she has trouble finding the correct one, guide her to it.

5 Repeat steps 3 and 4 with the rest of the shapes you have made. When your child is more confident, start again, and see if she can find the correct holes for the shapes on her own.

6 Once your child has become more familiar with the shapes you are using, start to introduce language. When you pass her the shape, say what it is, and relate it back to her knowledge of the way it feels. For example, "This is a triangle. The triangle has three sides."

Also try

Once this has been mastered, you can create variations in the size and shape of the holes and corresponding objects, ideally on the same box, so that the task presents your child with more of a challenge.

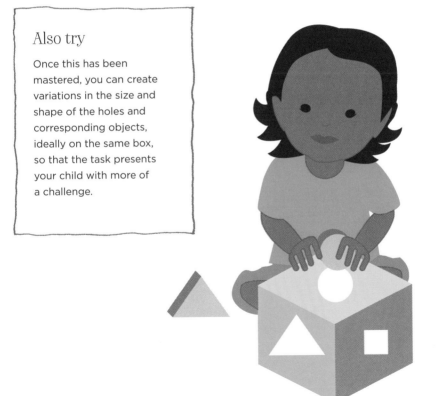

ROLL A BALL

While your toddler may not have yet developed the skills to catch a ball, he will be able to send and receive a ball in a rolling action as introduced in this next activity. It's a great activity for starting to develop those gross motor skills and hand–eye coordination.

You will need

- **Beach ball or similarly large, lightweight ball**

Before you roll the ball to him, briefly look down and then look at him so that he makes the association of looking to the sending point.

Activity

1   Sit on the floor with your legs apart so that you are face to face with your child

2   Invite your child to sit in the same way. By sitting like this you are defining an area and making a barrier for the ball.

3   Begin by gently rolling the ball toward your child.

4   Encourage him to stop the ball with his hands. If necessary you may need to demonstrate this.

5   Invite him to roll the ball back to you.

6   When he becomes confident in passing the ball, move yourself back a little farther. This step can be repeated again when he gains confidence at this new distance.

BEANBAG THROWING

Beanbags are one of the best pieces of equipment to help young children develop their throwing skills. Unlike a ball, beanbags won't roll away from them, so they feel nice and secure. In this activity the target area for throwing the beanbag is defined to help hand–eye coordination.

You will need

- Large indoor or outdoor space
- Jump rope or hoop
- Beanbag or bean-filled soft toy per child

Remind your child that she needs to keep her arm straight when throwing.

Activity

1 Lay the rope on the ground and shape it into a circle.

2 Stand about 20 in. (50 cm) away from the rope and demonstrate to your child how to throw the beanbag underarm into the target.

3 Let your child have a try.

4 Once she has mastered this distance, take a step back and let her try it again.

Also try

You could extend the activity by having colored cones and asking her to throw at a particular color.

If there is more than one child, they could see who is first to get their beanbag into the target.

RING TOSS GAME

Ring toss is a game that I am sure we all remember from our own childhoods and it is one of the best games for developing motor skills combined with eye–hand coordination. We always want our children to have the greatest chance of success, so for younger children particularly I have broken down the game into three stages. These steps make a natural progression in the refinement of skills and challenge level for your child. For the equipment, I would suggest bamboo sticks pushed into flowerpots filled with earth. Hoops are available from any good toy or sports store.

You will need

- 3 to 5 medium-size flowerpots filled with earth or sand
- 3 to 5 bamboo sticks
- 3 to 5 rings
- 3 to 5 dishpans or buckets
- Masking tape or a ball of string

Activity

1   Mark out three circles using your masking tape or string on the ground. About 15 to 20 in. (40 to 50 cm) across. Invite your child to see if he can get his hoops into each of the circles. When he has mastered this, move onto the next stage.

2 Place the dishpans into the circles. This time invite your child to see if he can get his hoops into the bowls. When he feels confident with this, move onto the next stage.

3 Remove the bowls and put a flowerpot into each circle. Push a stick into each flower pot with about 8 in. (20 cm) showing. Now invite your child to see if he can get his hoop over each stick.

Start with three targets and graduate to five.

For older children, you could start at stage 2 or 3.

Make a marker point for your child to stand at and move these farther back as he gains confidence at that distance.

Also try

This game could also be used as an excellent introduction to colors, using colored circles, bowls, and sticks. You could also introduce numbers in the same way, by numbering the targets and then you could combine the two. So, "See if you can get your hoop over the red, number 1 target."

CIRCUS PERFORMER

In some ways, balance is like a child's sixth sense. Young children seem to have within them an innate longing to develop their balance and they take any opportunity given to them to walk low beams or along low walls. This activity allows them to pretend to be a circus performer, walking a tightrope, but in complete safety.

You will need

- **Large outdoor space**
- **Piece of colored chalk**

Activity

1 Find a stone-paved or concrete area where the chalk can be rubbed off.

2 Draw a straight line about 10 ft. (3 m) long.

3 Demonstrate to your child how to walk along the line, putting one foot directly in front of the other. Walk with an upright position, eyes forward and arms stretched out horizontally.

4 Let your child have a turn, but he will need your support to guide him in a straight line, so keep hold of both of his outstretched hands as he walks along.

Also try

When he is confident walking the line, he could try holding two flags in each hand. He could also try carrying a small bell, which he has to try not to let ring when walking.

When your child is ready to progress to walking along a low beam or brick wall, let him choose the beam he wants to start with. Children have a very good sense of what height they feel comfortable with.

CIRCUS PERFORMER 2

Now that your child has mastered walking on the line, she is ready to try some other activities that will extend her balance and coordination. This series of activities uses the same line concept, but your child will also be required to hold things. The chosen objects are graduated in difficulty so that, once one object is mastered, she can progress onto the next one.

You will need

- Masking tape
- 2 beanbags or soft toys

Activity

1   Using the masking tape mark out a line about 10 ft. (3 m) long.

2   Remind your child about the first circus performer activity of keeping her balance while walking on a line. Let her practice this again.

3   Explain that this time she is going to try a new challenge; she will still walk on the line, but this time she will be holding two beanbags. Demonstrate this and then invite her to try.

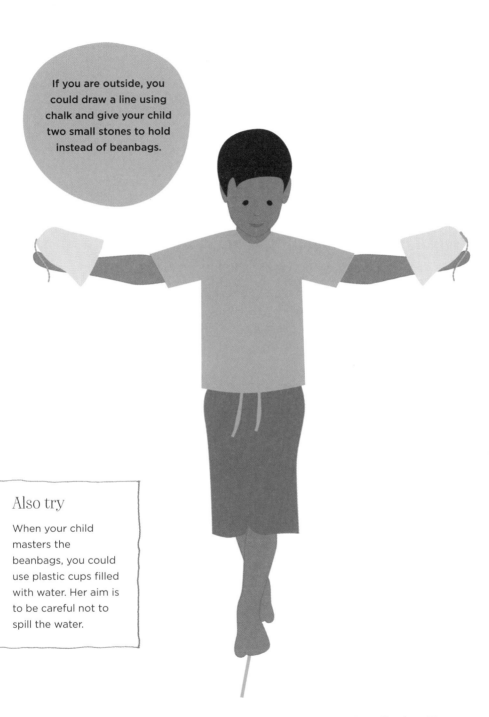

If you are outside, you could draw a line using chalk and give your child two small stones to hold instead of beanbags.

Also try

When your child masters the beanbags, you could use plastic cups filled with water. Her aim is to be careful not to spill the water.

TARGET BALL

Once your child has mastered sending and receiving a rolling ball, she will now be ready for "Target ball." The degree of coordination is greater, as not only does the ball need to be sent, but also, as the name implies, it has to be aimed at a target. The target is filled with water, which adds to the fun factor, but in reality helps to stop the ball from bouncing off target.

You will need

- Large bowl, like a dishpan, filled with about 4 in. (10 cm) water
- Large waterproof sheet (if playing the game indoors)
- Medium to large, lightweight ball

Activity

1 Place the bowl with the water on the floor. If playing the game indoors, lay down a waterproof sheet first to avoid water damage from splashes.

2 Stand close to the bowl with the ball in your hand and gently throw the ball into the bowl.

3 Pick up the ball and give it to your child. Invite her to try and throw it into the bowl.

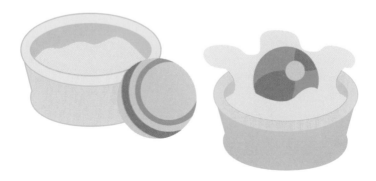

4 Once she has been able to reach this target, invite her to step farther back and to try throwing the ball from this new distance. This step can be repeated once she has reached the target from this new distance.

5 Once your child is able to do this from different distances, you can make the activity more challenging by introducing a small to medium-size bowl and ball, and repeating steps 1 to 4 with her.

Remember that all children take their own time to master a new skill and it may be that your child will not be able to achieve all the targets the first time.

BOWLING ALLEY

Your children can have their own bowling alley in their home with this very easy-to-prepare ninepins game. They will enjoy seeing the pins tumble as they hit them with a rolling ball. This game can be played individually, in pairs, or in teams. It's also a great game for improving hand–eye coordination.

You will need

- Long, narrow indoor or outdoor space, about 13 x 3 ft (4 x 1 m)
- 5 large, empty water or soda bottles with caps
- Medium-size, lightweight ball

You could decorate the bowling pins with colored stickers or number the pins with a colored marker.

If the pins seem a little unstable, you could fill them with some water or with rice to weigh them down.

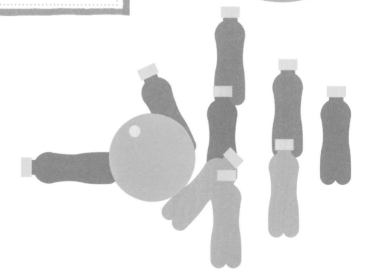

Activity

1 Set all of the bowling pins up in a row at one end of your chosen space.

2 Ask your children to stand at the other end.

3 You could line cushions down the sides of the alley to clearly define the path for the children.

4 Demonstrate to them how to roll the ball to try to knock down the pins.

5 Let them take turns trying to knock down the pins and helping to set them up again for the next player.

Also try

Once the children become more confident with this game and are able to knock down more of the pins, you could change the formation to make it more challenging for them.

DECORATE YOUR OWN HULA HOOP

A hula hoop has to be one of the most versatile children's toys, which can be used for a variety of games. In this activity your child will get to customize their hoop so it will be uniquely hers. I have chosen the classic spiral, but if your child is particularly creative there are plenty of suggested alternatives.

You will need

- Hula hoop
- Roll of metallic tape, any color
- Scissors
- Ribbon or string about 15³/₄ in. (40 cm) long

Also try

Here are some other patterns for you to try:

- Double or triple spiral
- Criss-cross
- Plaid: criss-cross pattern using different colored tapes with no gaps
- Rainbow: mark out seven even sections on the hoop for each of the colors and spiral wrap with no gaps

Activity

1 Place the hula hoop on the table along with the tape, scissors, and ribbon or string.

2 Invite your child to the table and explain to her that she is going to decorate her hula hoop.

3 Cut a length of tape about 8 in. (20 cm) long. Repeat with several more lengths of tape.

4 Using the ribbon or string, demonstrate by looping it around the hoop in a spiral; let her decide how big she would like the spaces on the spiral to be.

5 Stick the first length of tape around the hoop in a spiral.

6 Now invite your child to continue the spiral using the other pieces of tape until the spiral is complete around the hoop.

CHINESE JUMP ROPE

When I played this game as a child, two friends would act as the posts for the elastic and we would take turns to be the skipper. In this version, two chairs are used as posts, but if friends come over to play, your child can revert to the traditional way. In this activity we use a very simple sequence, but as your child masters this game he can learn more complex sequences.

You will need

- **Piece of elastic 16 to 23 ft. (5 to 7 m) long**
- **2 sturdy chairs**

For younger children, set the elastic at 4 in. (10 cm) from the floor.

Make sure the chairs are sturdy; if concerned, you could weigh the seats down.

Activity

1   Tie the two ends of the elastic together to form a loop.

2   Set your chairs about 16 ft. (5 m) from each other with backs facing.

3   Invite your child to help you put the elastic around the back set of legs of each chair (about 8 in. [20 cm] from the floor), to form a rectangle of elastic.

4   To demonstrate, stand with your legs astride one elastic, and then jump over to the other elastic and back. Let your child practice this.

5   Demonstrate again, this time with both feet in the middle. Jump out so your legs are astride both elastics and back again. Jump out once more, then jump on top of the two elastics.

6   Invite your child to have a go. Once he has managed this, see if he can put both sequences together.

Also try

As your child becomes confident with the game, move the elastic higher so the jumping requires more effort.

Here is a rhyme your child could say while doing the sequence:

Chocolate cake, when you bake,
How many minutes will you take?
One, two, three, four.

Your child could try doing it together with a friend.
Vary the sequence and rhymes; you can find many online.

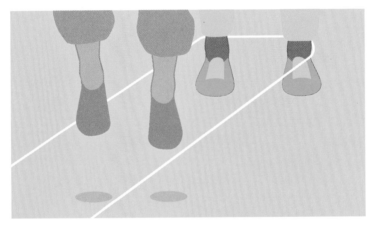

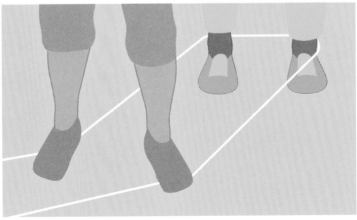

CAT'S CRADLE

Cat's cradle is one of the oldest games in recorded human history and there are references to it from different cultures across the world. The game is traditionally played with a partner with the string changing hands to form a different shape. In this activity, there are four different shapes that make the sequence. At first try, it will appear very tricky to your child, but once she has mastered it she will be delighted at her new skill.

You will need

- Yarn or string about 3 ft. (1 m) long

When introducing this activity, you could just start by repeating steps 1 and 2 and then work up to the next steps one by one.

Activity

1   Start by tying the end of the yarn together to form a loop.

2   Ask your child to hold out her hands 12 to 15 in. (30 to 40 cm) apart with palms facing each other.

3   Loop the yarn around each of her wrists once and ask her to pull the yarn taut.

4   Ask her to use her middle finger on her right hand to pull the thread of yarn from the left wrist across to the right. Ask her to repeat the same action using her left-hand, middle finger. The yarn makes a cross shape called "the cat's cradle."

5   Approaching from the side, place your thumb and index finger on both hands either side of the cross, pull outward and under the bottom string, then upward through the middle. At the same time, ask your child to release her fingers as you open out your thumbs and index fingers. You have now made the second shape, which is a horizontal cross.

6   Ask your child to grab either side of the two Xs using her thumb and index fingers on both hands, lift, pull out past the outer strings, under and upward through the middle, finally pulling out to form the next shape, which I call tram lines.

7   Next, using your little finger on your right hand, hook under the inner left string and pull out to the right to form a triangle. Repeat the same action with the little finger on the left hand to the right inner string, pulling to the left. You now have a diamond shape.

8   With your thumb and index finger on both hands (pushed together), go down through the triangles and up through the middle, keeping hold of the strings in your little fingers. Open up your thumb and index fingers while your child releases their fingers. You are now back at the cat's cradle and you can start the sequence again.

Be careful not to let go of the strings in the little fingers when making the final shape or the final shape will not work.

Also try

Once your child has mastered the sequence, she could introduce it to her friends and they could have a cat's cradle race.

RIBBON ON A STICK AND DANCE ROUTINE

In my twenty years plus of teaching children, I have yet to come across a child that did not enjoy moving to music. Your child may find jumping, skipping, hopping, or balancing tricky, but if you add music he can become so enraptured with dancing to the music that he forgets about the technical challenges of movement and learning a sequence. He will also enjoy trying to match his movements to that of the ribbon on the stick.

You will need

- **Ribbon or thin strip of crêpe paper about 3 ft. (1 m), tied to a stick**
- **Lively music with contrasting tempos**

For younger children needing more support, you could use a second stick for them to mirror your movements until they feel confident to move by themselves.

Activity

1 Show your child the ribbon on the stick and demonstrate by moving your arm in different shapes and directions to move the ribbon.

2 Pass the stick to your child and tell him that you are going to turn on some music so that he can move the ribbon in time with it.

3 As he starts moving to the music, suggest opposing movements such as moving slowly, quickly, jumping up high, crouching down low, spinning high, spinning low.

4 Add different ways of moving, such as baby steps, giant steps, skipping, galloping, hopping, jumping, twisting.

5 Ask your child to choose three of her favorite movements and put them together in a sequence.

6 Ask her to repeat the sequence of movements until she can link them together without any pauses. Tell her that she has now made up her own dance.

Also try

This activity is ideal for any number of children and perfect for when friends come to play.

The dance could have a theme such as animals. For an animal theme, try music such as *Peter and the Wolf* (by Sergei Prokofiev) or *Carnival of the Animals* (by Camille Saint-Saëns).

HOPSCOTCH

This is a win-win game in that it incorporates physical development of the gross motor skills, including balance and hand–eye coordination, plus learning how to write and sequence numbers. An all-round winner! You will need an outside area large enough to mark out the hopscotch grid.

You will need

- 2 pieces of white or colored chalk
- 2 small stones

Some children may struggle in particular with writing the number two; just observe this, and then help her practice the number at a later time.

Activity

1   Invite your child to help you mark out the hopscotch grid.

2   Using the chalk, draw a square. Ask your child what number comes first and ask her to write it into the square.

3   Above the number one square, draw two more equal-sized squares.

4   Ask your child to fill in the next two numbers.

5   Repeat the same steps until the grid is complete up to 10.

6   Demonstrate to her how to play by throwing your stone onto the number one, hopping on, picking up the stone, and hopping back. Continue to the number five and then invite her to have a turn.

Also try

For children who really enjoy numbers, you could extend the grid up to 20.

You could play the game jumping only on the even or odd numbers.

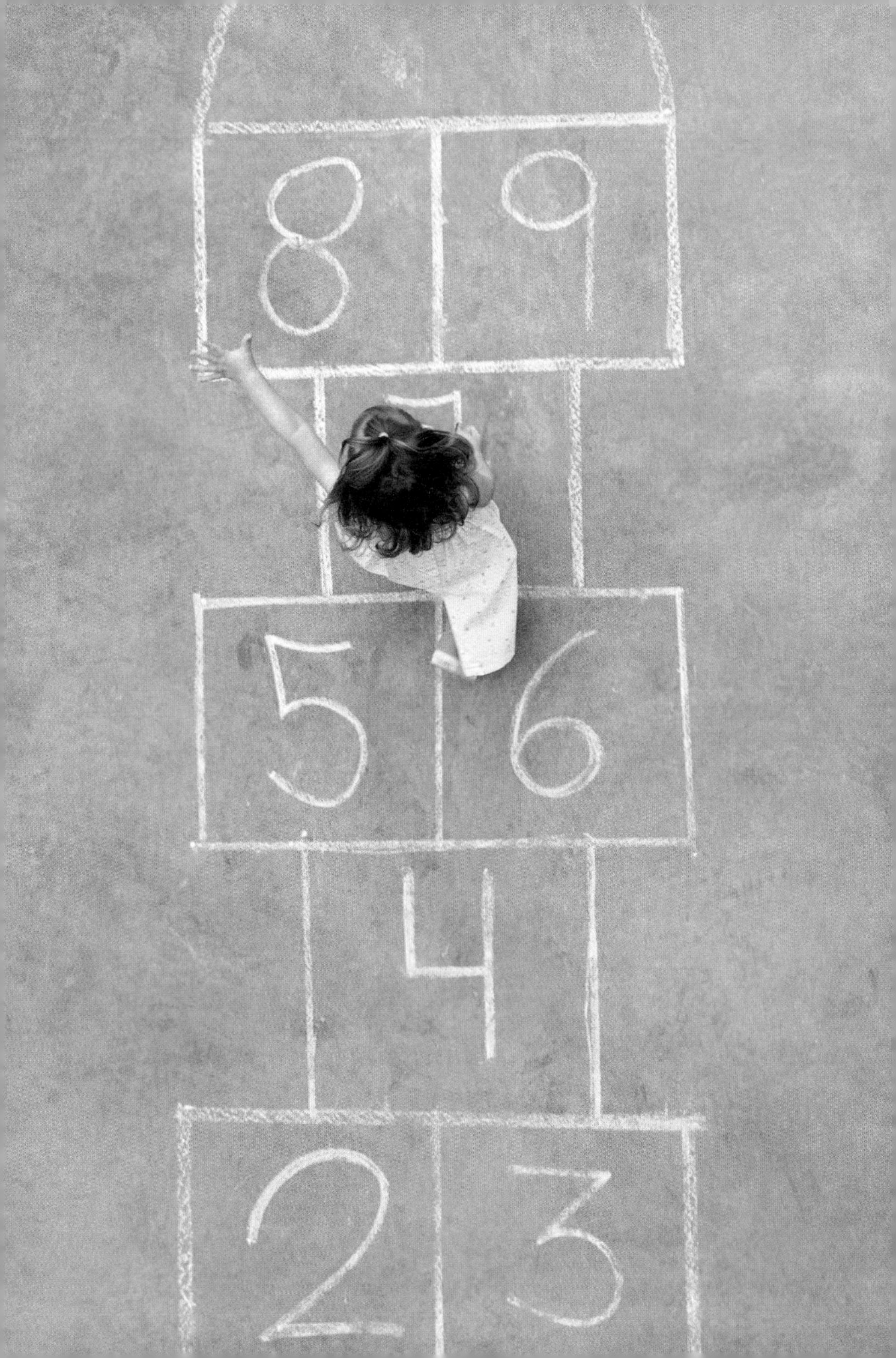
8
9
7
5
6
4
2
3

PICKUP STICKS

Adults and children alike will be familiar with this traditional game that tests hand-eye coordination and fine motor skills, plus nerves of steel and patience. I use the wooden skewers that you can buy from most grocery stores, but there are alternatives that you could use (see tip). For this first version while your child is learning how to play the game, the sticks are not colored.

You will need

- Pack of wooden skewers

Activity

1. Tell your child that you would like to show him a new, fun game called "pickup sticks."

2. Gather up the sticks into one bundle and then drop them to fall naturally on the floor.

3. Explain to your child that they need to pick up a stick without any of the other sticks moving, then he will gain a point.

4. Pick up a stick and then invite your child to do the same.

5. Remind your child that if another stick moves he is not allowed a point.

6. Keep playing the game until all the sticks have gone.

Safety point: skewers have sharp ends so please ensure your child is made aware of these and supervised when playing.

Also try

Once your child has understood the rules of the game, you could color the sticks by painting them or soaking them briefly in food coloring. Each color could represent a number of points.

Once your child has mastered this game, he could introduce it to his friends.

JACKS

The game of jacks has a history that is believed to derive from either ancient Greece or ancient Egypt, when it was known as "five stones" or "jackstones." The game's appeal is its simplicity, as it can be enjoyed by all generations. It develops hand–eye coordination, memory, and concentration. In addition, there is a mathematical element with the number of jacks to be collected.

You will need

- **10 small items such as jacks or stones**
- **Small bouncy ball**

Activity

1   Invite your child to observe your demonstration of the game. Begin by throwing the jacks or stones as if rolling dice.

2   Toss up the ball, pick up a jack, and, before the ball bounces for a second time, catch the ball, all with one hand.

3   Invite your child to have a go and let her practice several times.

4   The first round is known as "onesies." The picked-up jack is transferred to the opposite hand and the jacks are continued to be picked up one at a time until 10 is reached.

5   Let your child continue picking up the jacks, one at a time.

6   The next round is known as "twosies," where two jacks are picked up at a time, then three, four, etc. In the case of numbers of six or more, the remaining jacks do not need to be picked up.

Also try

You can make different rules for how many times the ball can bounce before picking up the jack, which can be useful if children are learning the game.

For children who may have difficulty with the catching aspect, play with five jacks instead of 10.

WEAVING AROUND A BANISTER

The action of weaving in and out is fundamental to a variety of different activities that will help your child's hand–eye coordination, development, and at the same time strengthen his finger and wrist muscles. Weaving around the banister is an excellent place to start because, due to the large scale, your child will clearly see the pattern that weaving your material in and out produces.

You will need

- Lengths of ribbon or strips of fabric, such as a cut up sheet, about 3 ft. (1 m) long.
- A length of banister about 3 ft. (1 m) long.

Activity

1 Choose a length of banister that is ideally flat along a landing. If your child is right-handed, he should be sitting on your left but well away from the drop of the stairs (reverse this if your child is left-handed).

2 Explain to your child that you are going to show him how to weave. Take a length of ribbon and tie the end onto the banister pole on your left about 3 ft. (1 m) away from you.

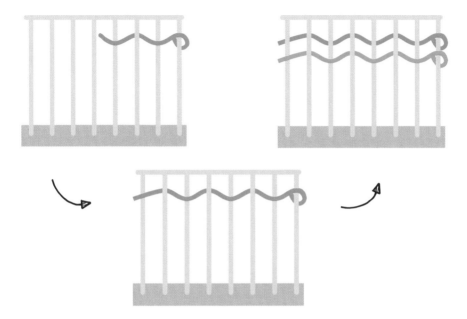

3 Now weave the ribbon in and out until you reach the end.

4 Untie the ribbon and invite your child to have a go.

5 Once he has mastered the weaving action, select another ribbon and repeat but starting a little higher up.

Also try

Try a variety of fabrics to weave, from crêpe paper to yarn. Try weaving your materials into a color pattern. Once your child has mastered the banisters, he could try weaving shoe laces in and out of a tennis racket's strings.

If he doesn't get the weaving action straight away, simply carry out the demonstration again.

CARDBOARD TUBE THREADING

Here's another excellent, simple activity that your child will find endlessly absorbing and will provide another opportunity for developing hand–eye coordination and strengthening finger muscles. It also has the added advantage of being very easy to prepare.

You will need

- Small bell, tennis ball, or any small object wider than the end of the tube
- Chain or cord about 3 ft. (1 m) long (you could even use the cord from a bathrobe)
- Knife to cut the tube
- Cardboard tube (the type you have on the inside of a paper towel roll)

Activity

1 Start by tying the bell or small object to one end of the chain. This will act as a stop for the tube and prevent it from coming off the chain.

2 Put the chain on the floor or a low table.

3 Cut the tube in half.

4 Demonstrate to your child how to thread the tube onto the chain and slide it back and forth.

5 Remove the tube from the chain and allow your child to have a try.

When demonstrating this activity, your child needs to sit to the left of you so that she can have an unrestricted view of your hands. If your child is left-handed you will need to demonstrate with your left hand, and your child will also need to sit on the right side of you.

Also try

Once the threading with the cardboard tube has been mastered try using thread spools threaded onto a shoelace.

You could also try threading fallen leaves onto picture wire.

PASTA THREADING

When your child has mastered "Cardboard tube threading,"
she is now ready to move onto pasta threading, which requires
a greater degree of fine motor skills.

You will need

- **Several pieces of string, approximately 20 in. (50 cm) long**
- **Packet of rigatoni pasta (tube shapes)**

Activity

1 Put out the pieces of string and pasta either on a low table or on the floor.

2 Invite your child to join you and explain that you are going to show her how to thread the pasta tubes onto the string.

3 Take a piece of pasta and thread it onto the string. When you get a few inches from the end, tie a knot in the string so that the first piece of pasta acts as a stop for the rest of the chain.

4 Demonstrate to your child how to thread a piece of pasta onto the string.

5 Now give her a piece of pasta to thread.

6 Let her continue threading the pasta until the string is full.

When you first try this activity with your child, make sure to choose the largest tube-shaped pasta that is available.

You could make your string of pasta into jewelry—all you need is some food coloring.

Activity

1 Add a teaspoon of food coloring to a bowl or deep baking sheet filled with water.

2 Holding both ends of the pasta string, pass it to your child and explain that she needs to dip it into the colored water so that the pasta is covered.

3 Remind her that she needs to keep hold of the string.

4 Keep the pasta in the water for a couple of minutes so that it is stained with the color.

5 Ask her to remove the pasta from the water.

6 Take the pasta string and hang it up to dry, putting a sheet of paper underneath to catch any drips.

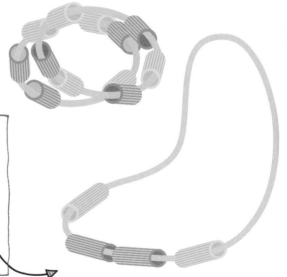

Also try

You could do two strings of pasta, each of a different color. When both strings have dried, they can be rethreaded onto a new string to make a necklace of two different colors.

THREADING BUTTONS WITH A PIPE CLEANER

Of all the hand-eye coordination activities I can think of, this has got to be one of my favorites. Not only does it develop children's coordination, but also their concentration. I have seen the youngest of children totally absorbed and content for sustained periods of time. It is almost as though it fulfills a deep need in them. In addition, I like the fact that there are so many variations and levels of skills. Threading using a pipe cleaner is an excellent place to start as the stiffness of the pipe cleaner requires less guidance than using, for example, a shoelace.

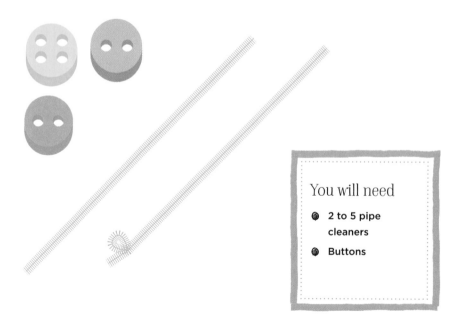

You will need

- 2 to 5 pipe cleaners
- Buttons

> Pipe clearners come in different shapes and sizes—make sure the holes on your buttons are going to be large enough before starting this project.

Also try

Ask your child if he is able to make a pattern with his buttons on the pipe cleaner.

After pipe cleaners, you could try threading using picture wire, shoelaces, or string. See activity on page 160.

You could use beads, rolled up pieces of silver foil, chopped up straws, or dried pasta.

Activity

1 Explain to your child that you would like to show him some threading activities.

2 Choose one of the pipe cleaners and roll up a little of one of the ends to make a small ball.

3 Offer a pipe cleaner to your child so that he can make a small ball at one end.

4 Thread a button onto your pipe cleaner and invite your child to choose a button to thread.

5 Once you have seen that he has understood what is required, let him work independently.

FLYING FISH

This game combines two activities in one. First, your child makes and designs her fish, then she learns how to propel it with the aid of a newspaper. If there is more than one child, or if you make one as well, you can race the fish.

You will need

- **Picture of a fish like the one to the right, photocopy one for each child**
- **Colored pencils, crayons, or markers**
- **Scissors**
- **Rolled-up newspaper or magazine for each child**

Activity

1   Explain that you are going to make some flying fish.

2   Give your child a photocopy of the fish and ask her to color it in.

3   Help your child to cut out the fish.

4   Put a finished fish onto a noncarpeted floor.

5   Using a rolled-up newspaper or magazine, demonstrate how to propel the fish along by beating the air behind it.

6   Let your child have a try.

7   Once she has managed to propel her fish, organize all the fish along a starting line to have a fish race.

Remember to use a noncarpeted floor. Wood or laminate is best.

TRANSFERRING LIQUID WITH A BASTER

Think of the countless times over the course of a day that you use your thumb and index finger and you will begin to realize how much the muscles in those fingers are essential. This activity helps your child to develop and strengthen these muscles by using a turkey baster to transfer liquid from container to container. As well as developing hand–eye coordination it acts as an excellent preparation for developing those muscles that will be used when your child comes to write.

You will need

- **2 glasses or clear plastic cups**
- **Small tray**
- **Food coloring, any color**
- **Baster**

Activity

1   Ask your child to half fill one of the glasses with water and then place it on the tray.

2   Ask him to place the empty glass on the tray a small distance away from the other glass.

3   Put a few drops of food coloring into the water.

4   Show him the baster and demonstrate how it works with the colored water in the glass. Invite him to try using the same glass.

5   Explain that he now needs to try to transfer the colored water into the empty glass. Give him a short demonstration and invite him to try.

6   When all the colored water has been transferred, then he may repeat the activity.

Also try

You could add another glass, up to four in total.

When the baster has been mastered you could try using a pipette and exchange the glasses for egg cups.

Using a tray helps to define an area (opt for plain rather than patterned) and makes cleaning easier in case of spills.

MATCHING
NUTS AND BOLTS

This activity uses the same thumb and index finger twisting action as the "Opening and closing objects" activity on page 156 but with a smaller and more refined action. Your child will have to use her judgment to work out the correct size of nut to fit the bolt.

You will need

- 8 nuts
- 8 matching bolts
- Tray, preferably plain

Activity

1   Put the nuts and bolts on the tray on the table.

2   Invite your child to the table and tell her that you have a new activity to show her.

3   Set out the eight bolts in a row with the nuts in a row below.

Small parts can be a choking hazard, so this activity should not be attempted by a child under the age of three.

4 Demonstrate by selecting one of the nuts and one of the bolts and seeing if they fit together. When you find the matching nut and bolt, screw the nut onto the bolt. Now choose another nut and repeat this step.

5 Unscrew the two nuts and bolts, put them back in the rows, and then mix the rows.

6 Invite your child to do the activity, matching and threading all the nuts and bolts.

Also try

For role play you could set up a workshop.

You could show your child the difference between a nut, a bolt, and a screw, and how to use a screwdriver.

SORTING NUTS AND BOLTS USING A MAGNET

Children are endlessly fascinated by nuts and bolts and magnets, which are employed in this activity to teach your child to sort metal objects into different sizes using a magnet. A steady hand and focused concentration is required, along with a sharp eye to spot the different-size bolts and nuts.

You will need

- Tray, preferably plain
- Nuts and bolts of various sizes
- 4 to 6 containers
- Large magnet

When first introducing this activity, start with only three or four different containers and spread the nuts and bolts far apart. As the activity is mastered, bring them closer together and work up to six containers.

Activity

1 Invite your child to the table and tell her that you would like to show her a new, fun game.

2 Put the tray in front of your child and pour on the nuts and bolts, spreading them apart.

3 Line up the containers in a row just outside the top of the tray.

4 Pick up the magnet and use it to lift up one of the bolts, and then place the bolt into one of the containers. Invite her to do the same, saying that she needs to find the same size bolt.

5 When all bolts of one size have been sorted, move onto one size of the nuts.

6 Continue in this way until all the nuts and bolts have been sorted into all the containers.

Also try

Investigate which objects in your house use nuts and bolts.

Go on a magnet hunt to discover what objects in your house are magnetic.

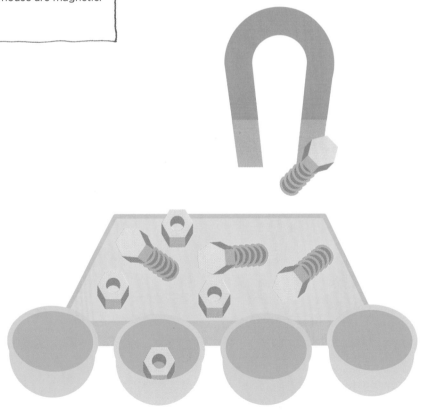

LIFE SKILLS

The activities in this chapter will equip your child with important life skills. To an adult, these tasks may appear simple because they are carried out automatically. But your child will experience a sense of accomplishment and self-worth when she is able to carry out these activities independently.

The first group of activities teach basic personal hygiene, such as washing hands and brushing hair. Further activities include putting on shoes and learning to pour, which have the benefit of helping your child develop hand–eye coordination.

WASHING HANDS

What could be more fundamental than washing and drying your hands? And yet many children start school without this skill. Imagine how proud and confident your child will feel if she knows how to wash her hands when asked to do so. Using a sink can be quite tricky for a child at first; start with a bowl of water, as explained here.

You will need

- Large plastic bowl
- Bar of soap on a soap dish or pump soap dispenser
- Medium pitcher filled with warm water
- 2 hand towels
- Tray

Activity

1 Place the bowl on the tray with the other items to the right (or left, if your child is left-handed). Half-fill the bowl with water.

2 Wet your hands and rub soap over your hands slowly so that your child can see that you are covering your hands with the soap. Place the soap back on the dish or, if you are using a pump dispenser, remind your child that you only need one or two squirts.

When your child has mastered washing her hands, explain why and when we need to wash our hands. After using the toilet, before meals, and before cooking, remind your child to wash her hands, until she remembers for herself. Remember to lead by example!

3 Rinse your hands in the water. Dry your hands using a towel—again slowly, so your child can see you drying all parts of your hands.

4 As you replace the dirty water with clean water, ask your child why the water needs to be changed before she washes her hands. Show her the dirty water as a clue. Invite your child to try for herself.

Also try

Show your child how to wash her hands at a sink. With your child standing on a stool, show her how to: put in the plug; turn on the faucet (a quarter turn) and turn them off again; check the temperature of the water; pull out the plug when finished.

Show your child how to cover her mouth when coughing and explain why this is important.

BRUSHING TEETH

If ever there was a good habit that should be learned at an early age, then brushing teeth is it. Explain when we need to brush our teeth, including after meals and bedtime. Take this opportunity to explain why we don't share toothbrushes and towels.

You will need

- 2 toothbrushes
- Large plastic bowl
- 2 cups
- Tube of toothpaste
- Face mirror on a stand
- Medium pitcher filled with water
- 2 hand towels
- Tray

Activity

1   Put out the materials, with the mirror in the center. Half-fill one cup with water and put it to the right of the bowl. Keep your child's toothbrush, cup, and towel on the tray, and place out of reach until it is his turn.

2   Release the top of the toothpaste tube and squeeze out a small amount (no bigger than the size of a pea).

3   Brush your teeth and gums slowly, while looking in the mirror. This will help your child to understand how to use the mirror.

4   Rinse out your mouth with water from the cup. With the remaining water, pour over the toothbrush and clean the bristles. Wipe your mouth with a towel.

5   Bring your child's materials forward and make sure they are set out in the same positions you had before.

> When your child needs to brush his teeth again, take him to the sink and repeat the task there.

BRUSHING HAIR

Both boys and girls are fascinated by the task of brushing hair.
I have watched children absorbed in this activity, not through
vanity, but through satisfaction of a skill mastered and
taking pride in their appearance.

You will need

- Face mirror on a stand
- 2 hairbrushes (one for you, one for your child)

Activity

1   Place the mirror in the center of the table. Put your brush in front of the mirror and your child's brush out of the way.

2   Brush your hair with slow, gentle strokes, turning your head so that you brush both sides. Use the mirror and explain what you are doing.

3   Move the mirror so your child can see and set the brush in front of the mirror for your child to try.

Also try

Show your child how to make a ponytail and how to plait long hair, using a doll.

USING A NAILBRUSH

This exercise is all about introducing a new movement. Brushing from side to side while keeping the nails steady inside the bristles is a tricky task to master for little hands. It encourages your child to meditate on her hands, concentrating on how the bubbles and water feels.

You will need

- **Child-size nailbrush made from natural bristles and wood**
- **Pitcher containing warm water and a bowl to pour it into**
- **Bar of soap**
- **Towel**

Activity

1 If you have a low table, place the pitcher and basin on top, next to the soap, nailbrush, and towel.

2 Tell your child that she is going to make her hands and nails really clean.

3 Get her to pour some water into the basin. Encourage her to realize when there is enough water.

4 Pick up the nailbrush. Demonstrate how to pick up some soap on the brush, wet the brush, and then apply the brush to her fingertips in a sideways motion.

5 Encourage your child to do the same, making sure that she focuses on how the brush feels on her fingers. This should be a calm, meditative exercise.

6 Now, both wash off the soap from your hands, rubbing and rinsing them well in your bowl of warm water.

7 When all the soap is rinsed off, get your child to pick up the towel and carefully dry off each finger and palm.

FOLDING CLOTHES

This activity begins very simply with folding handkerchiefs, and then moves on to folding clothes. When selecting clothes for your child to fold, choose clothes that have seams that could act as a guideline, for example, a shirt or sweater. Take the opportunity to explain why we need to fold clothes and, once folded, where clothes need to be kept. You could even stick pictures of clothing on different drawers as a reminder.

You will need

- **Old handkerchiefs**
- **Marker**
- **Ruler**
- **Selection of your child's clothes**
- **Large basket**

Activity

1   Mark an old handkerchief, using the marker pen, with a vertical and horizontal line. Put the handkerchief and clothes to be folded in the basket.

2 Take the handkerchief from the basket and place it flat on the table. Fold it along the marker lines. Open out the handkerchief and pass it to your child to try.

3 Repeat the exercise again, but use a handkerchief with no marker guidelines.

4 Move on to folding the clothes. Take one item of clothing at a time. Fold in the way of your choice, but aim to be consistent so your child can copy. If you fold over a right sleeve first, always start this way, whether folding a shirt or sweater.

Also try

Put folded clothes away in drawers and closets. Practice this with your child each time you do some laundry.

MAKING YOUR BED

For some children, the bedtime routine can induce anxiety.
Encouraging your child to become responsible for making his bed
can go some way toward reducing this anxiety. In addition,
it will help develop his hand–eye coordination skills.

You will need

- **Unmade bed**
- **Your child's favorite toy**

Activity

1 Invite your child to come to the unmade bed.

2 Suggest to him that his favorite toy (name the toy) does not look comfortable in the unmade bed and that he is going to make the bed so that it is more comfortable.

3 Start by asking him to remove the pillows and toy and place them on the floor.

4 Shake out the comforter or blanket and smooth down. Ask him to try to repeat this action.

5 Pick up the pillows, plump, replace on the bed, and smooth down. Ask him to repeat this action.

6 Ask him to return the toy and say that it looks a lot happier in the bed now.

Shaking out the comforter is quite a tricky action, so just observe how he does this; a second demonstration may be required at a later date.

Also try

The natural progression for this activity would be helping to put on the clean bed linen. Start with the pillowcases and then, with an adult's help, the sheets. Removing the linen that needs to be washed can be fun, too.

SOCK PAIRING GAME

Take your family's washed socks (not more than four pairs to begin with) and place in a basket. Now ask your child to find each matching sock, and to place one on top of the other to a make a pair. When all the socks are matched, show your child how to roll them up and fold them over to make into a ball.

You will need

- 4 or more pairs of matching socks
- Basket to store the socks in before and after the game

Activity

1 Begin by preparing the materials for the activity, putting the separated pairs of socks into a basket.

2 Explain to your child about the need to match socks so that you always wear the same style pair.

3 Present the activity to your child in the exact order in which you expect your child to complete it.

4 Remove the socks from the basket and place them on the floor or table one at a time, from left to right.

5 Encourage your child to look at the differences between the socks, such as sizes, colors, and textures.

6 Match each sock by placing the pairs on top of each other, keeping each pile separate.

7 Finally, show your child how to roll the pair together by rolling one sock into another, before inviting your child to try.

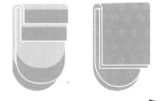

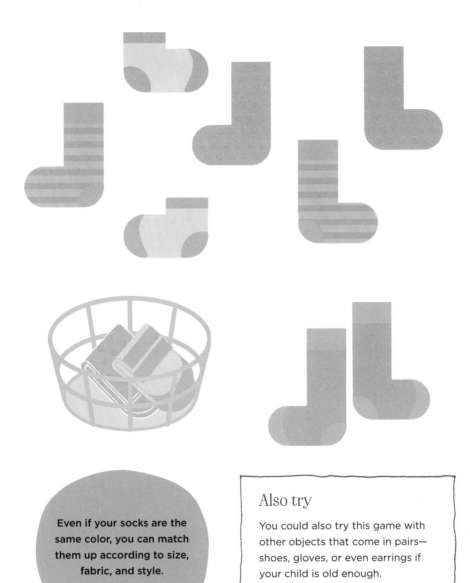

Even if your socks are the same color, you can match them up according to size, fabric, and style.

Also try

You could also try this game with other objects that come in pairs—shoes, gloves, or even earrings if your child is old enough.

PUTTING ON A JACKET

Here is a quick and fun way for your child to put on a coat or jacket by herself. It can take a while for her to understand the coordination required but, once mastered, she will really enjoy getting ready to go out.

For younger children, demonstrate putting on a coat yourself so they can watch. It may also be helpful to practice the movement without the coat.

Activity

1   Put the coat on the floor, inside facing up.

2   Ask your child to stand facing the neck end of the coat.

3   Ask her to squat down and put her arms down the sleeves.

4   As she stands up, ask her to swing her arms up and over her head, to finish with her arms by her sides and the coat on.

Also try

Using a favorite sweater, practice turning the sleeves the right-side out. Move on to whole items of clothing.

BUTTONING A SHIRT

This is a complex activity that has been broken down into easy stages so your child can understand each stage. One of the main difficulties children have with this skill is ensuring that the ends of the shirt are lined up so that they don't run out of buttonholes. To avoid this problem, this activity teaches buttoning with the shirt on a table and it is buttoned from the bottom to the top. This encourages your child to match up the bottom button with the bottom hole when fastening a shirt while wearing it.

You will need

- **Shirt (or cardigan) with large buttons**

Activity

1 Place the shirt on the table so your child can see clearly.

2 Open up the shirt and close it again, so your child can see how it works.

3 Starting at the bottom, guide the bottom button through the first hole slowly.

4 Open up the buttonhole as wide as possible so your child can see that it needs to be open for the button to pass through.

5 Finish the rest of the buttons and then undo them. Pass the shirt over for your child to try.

Also try

Practice with other clothes. Open and close each garment before fastening, and work from bottom to top. Move on to items with smaller buttons.

Try items with snaps and other fastenings. Make each movement clear to follow, and follow the same procedure as for the buttons.

Check that your child is confident putting on mittens or gloves and other items of clothing.

You could try using one of your own shirts, cardigans, or coats that has bigger buttons and then progress to one of his own shirts.

Make sure the shirt is not new or just washed.

ZIPPERS AND OTHER FASTENINGS

Children find zippering interesting, but very tricky. You may need to hold the bottom of zippers while they do the zippering action. This exercise will teach your child to both zip and unzip a garment, as each requires separate skills.

You will need

- Garment with a simple zipper fastening, or a specially designed zipper frame

Activity

1   Show your child the zipper already done up. Place your right thumb under the zipper handle and place your right index finger over to pinch the fingers together.

2   Pinch the top part of the material to the right of the zipper's teeth with your left thumb and index finger.

3   Slowly, and in a continuous movement, pull the zipper down, slowing down at the bottom to demonstrate clearly where the zipper pin comes out, then pull the two sides apart to emphasize the movement.

4   To zip the garment back together, pinch the handle with your right thumb and index finger, making sure that it's clear that the handle should be pointing down.

5   Place your right index finger on the top part of the tab and your right thumb at the bottom of the tab, then press firmly together.

6   Pinch the bottom part to the right of the zipper's teeth with your left thumb and index finger and slide the pin slowly into the tab, making sure it is fully in.

7   Repinch the zipper handle with your right thumb and index finger, pulling the material taught with your left hand, then slide the handle up until you reach the top.

LEARNING LEFT AND RIGHT SHOES

Learning the difference between left and right is linked to our concept of laterality—the idea that there is an internal self-awareness of left and right sides of the body, and a definite midway line that divides our body in half. Learning how to tell the left and right shoe apart will help your child develop this awareness, and this exercise will help her to recognize which shoe is which and help her to get dressed by herself.

You will need

- Pair of your child's shoes
- Marker, or a picture sticker cut in half
- Tray

Activity

1 Place the pair of shoes on a tray on a table, with the toes facing away from you both.

2 If your child can recognize her name, write one half of the letters on one shoe, and the other letters on the other shoe

3 Alternatively, if she can't yet read her own name, draw a smiley face in two halves, close to the inner edges of each shoe.

4 Show her the inside of the shoe, explaining that when she puts on her shoes, she needs to make sure that the face is smiling at her.

5 Place the shoes in random order on the floor and get her to work out which shoe goes on which foot.

You can buy, or make, your own stickers—but always make sure they line up with the inner edges of the shoe.

Also try

To help children learn the difference between left and right in general, show them this clever trick: Hold up their left hand, and make their thumb sit at right angles to the fingers, making an "L" shape. Tell them that this stands for left and if they ever get confused, to hold up their hands to see which one makes the "L" shape.

PUTTING ON SHOES

If your child is finding it difficult to put on his shoes, teach her how to do it when she is not wearing them, as explained here. Once your child has mastered these exercises, turn the shoes around with the heels pointing toward her to try.

Also try

She can then try with the shoes on her feet!

Tying laces is very difficult for a young person. Start with Velcro and other fastenings to encourage your child's confidence, and move on to trying laced shoes once she has mastered these.

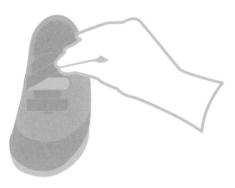

Velcro shoes

1. Ask your child to put the shoes onto a mat on the table with the toe ends facing you.

2. Bring the right shoe forward, lift up the straps, and place them so that your child can see that the straps must match up. Bring down the left shoe and put back the right shoe. Repeat with the left shoe.

3. Pass the shoes on the mat for your child to try.

Buckled shoes

1. Ask your child to put the shoes on to a mat on the table with the toe ends facing you. Starting with the right shoe, lift up the strap and thread under and up through the buckle.

2. Bend the strap back to reveal the holes. Push the pin into the hole and finish buckling the shoe.

3. Repeat with the left shoe, but turn it around so the heel is facing you. Unbuckle the shoes and pass them on the mat for your child to try.

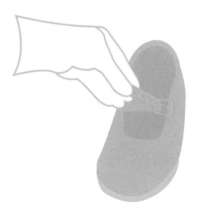

TYING LACED SHOES

Laced shoes can be quite a challenge for young children. Once your child has mastered putting on shoes with other fastenings, and is comfortable with identifying right and left shoes, you can move on to teaching her how to tie shoelaces.

Activity

1   Ask your child to put the shoes onto a mat on the table with the toe ends facing you. Take the right shoe, and place the laces out to the sides. Cross over both laces.

2   Take the right side lace with your right hand. Cross under the center join and pull on both ends to knot.

3   Take the left side lace with your left hand and slide your left hand down until you reach the middle of the lace. Pick it up between your thumb and second finger, and transfer it to your right hand, while your left hand holds the lace in the center to make a rabbit ear.

4   Take the right lace in the right hand, loop over the center section and pull through to tie a bow.

5   Repeat with the other shoe. Untie both shoelaces and pass the shoes over for your child to try.

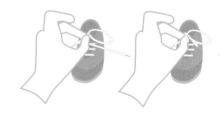

POLISHING SHOES

All children love this activity and the children in my class have
often offered to clean my shoes. In their enthusiasm for the task,
they have polished the soles, rendering walking a dangerous affair!
Polishing also helps to develop and refine fine motor skills. Safety point:
the use of shoe polish needs to be supervised. If consumed,
it could cause acute stomach problems.

You will need

- Can of neutral-colored polish
- Small container to hold a scoop of polish
- Table knife
- Plastic mat
- Child's leather shoes
- Small shoe brush
- Small cloth
- Tray

Activity

1   Before you ask your child to sit down, scoop out a small amount of polish and put it in the container. (This is to limit the amount of polish used.) Spread out the mat on the tray and add the shoes, polish container, brush, and cloth and invite your child to join you.

2   Pick up the cloth, take some of the polish and apply it to one shoe. Spread it evenly over the surface.

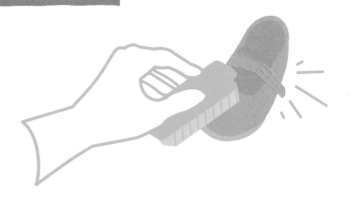

3 Return the cloth to the tray and pick up the brush. Use a buffing action to shine the shoe.

4 After the activity, you could ask your child why it is that we need to clean our shoes and why we need to put a mat out to put our shoes on. If he is not sure, guide him to the answer by showing him the bottom of his shoes.

Also try

Try the same activity but polish small wooden objects using furniture polish.

Show your child how to polish a low, wooden table.

LEARNING TO POUR

Stop and think how many times you use a pouring action during the day. This uncomplicated movement is easy for an adult, but for a child, learning how to pour requires intense concentration and hand–eye coordination. A great way for your child to master this skill is to try pouring beans from one large plastic pitcher to another. Once she is confident doing this, try the same activity using different substances.

You will need

- 2 plastic pitchers
- Packet of dried beans or lentils
- Tray

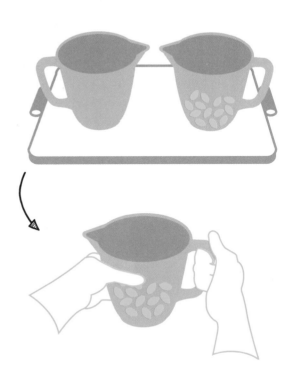

Activity

1   Put the pitchers on the tray with the spouts facing each other and the handles facing out. Fill the pitcher on the right a third full with dried beans or lentils.

2   Pick up the pitcher on the right with your right hand, supporting it with your left hand, as shown.

3   Pour the beans into the pitcher on the left. Now swap over the pitchers and invite your child to try the activity.

Also try

Replace the beans with finer substances, such as rice or sugar.

Try the same activity using water colored with a few drops of food coloring. (You will need a cloth to wipe up any spills.)

Instead of pouring from pitcher to pitcher, try pouring from a pitcher into cups.

Buy a play crockery set and add beans or lentils, etc.

For a real challenge, give your child a pitcher half-filled with water and let her pour the water into glasses for the dinner table.

LEARNING TO TRANSFER

Activities that involve transferring substances, such as spooning and pouring, help develop muscular coordination, which helps with eating, serving food for oneself and others, and cooking activities. They also prepare the muscles for the more complex task of writing. As with the pouring activities, this activity begins with a less refined substance moving to a finer substance.

You will need

- 2 small, shallow pots (about the size of a cupcake)
- Teaspoon
- Small tray
- Rice to half-fill one pot

Activity

1 Set out the two pots on the tray with the spoon on the right. Put the rice in the pot on the left.

2 Pick up the spoon and begin to transfer the rice from the left to right pot, until the pot is empty.

3 Swap the pots over so the pot with the rice is back on your left, with the spoon on the right. Pass the tray over for your child to try.

Always work from left to right. This helps prepare your child for reading.

If you take great care when transferring, your child will do the same.

If your child is left-handed, hold your spoon in the left hand.

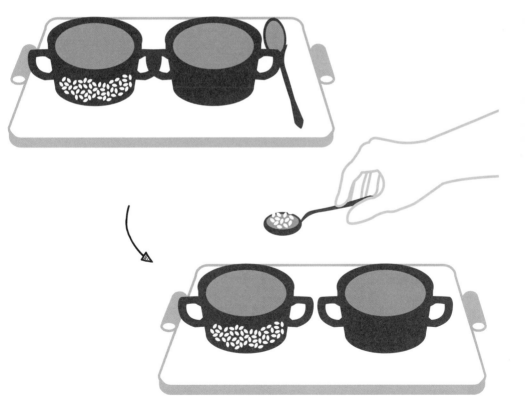

MAKING YOUR OWN PLACEMAT

This is a lovely creative project for your child before he masters setting the table. I suggest a fruit design as most children feel confident drawing fruit shapes; however, if your child has a particular passion, then use that for the design. This project's purpose is to make mealtimes a happy experience.

You will need

- Pencil
- Sheet of 8.5 x 11 in. white card
- Pictures of fruit (or other images)
- Apron
- Assortment of poster or acrylic paints in different colors
- Paint tray or paper plate
- Scissors
- Small piece of kitchen sponge
- Laminator or self-adhesive plastic

Activity

1   Show your child the pictures of the fruit, talk about the shapes, and get him to trace them with his finger. Show him how to put on his apron.

2   Ask him which fruit he would like to start with, and then place some suitable color paints on the tray or plate.

3   Explain to him that he is going to use his finger as a painting tool by dipping it into the paint.

4   Start him drawing the outline of the fruit and then fill it in, ensuring that there are spaces between the fingerprints.

5   For the leaves, cut out leaf shapes from a sponge, dip into green paint, and use as a stamp.

6   When the painting is finished and dry, laminate or cover with clear self-adhesive plastic.

Put out several shades of one color as well as white. Encourage your child to dip his finger into all the shades but try to avoid mixing up the colors.

Also try

Older children might like to add a fruit bowl to their picture.

Instead of using paint, you could make a collage with the pictures of fruit.

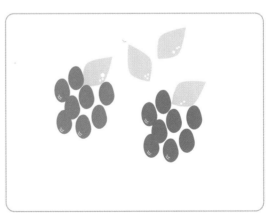

SETTING THE TABLE

Here is a quick and effective activity that will teach your child how to set the table. Using a sheet of paper with the place setting drawn on, your child will learn the positions of the cutlery and plate. Once he has mastered this skill, it could become his family job. Many children also enjoy being shown elaborate ways of folding a napkin. As well as the practical benefits, this activity reinforces folding, and right- and left-handed positions.

You will need

- Small plate to fit on the sheet of paper
- 8.5 x 11 in. sheet of thick paper
- Pencil
- Black marker
- Table knife
- Fork
- Spoon
- Tray

Before you ask your child to sit down, put the plate in the middle of the paper, and draw around it with the pencil. Follow the same steps for the cutlery, so that you have an outlined place setting on the paper. Go over the pencil outlines in marker to make them stand out.

Activity

1 Put the sheet of paper onto a tray along with the cutlery and plate. Ask your child to take the tray to the table and put it in front of him in the middle. Remove the paper and put it in front of the tray.

2 Say to your child, "I am going to match up the plate to the one on the paper." Trace around the rim of the plate with one finger and then repeat the action on the paper outline, so that your child will see that the shape matches.

3 Say to your child, "Can you match up the cutlery with the outlines on the paper sheet?" Spread the cutlery out on the tray so he can clearly see each item. Encourage him to match up the sheet and items.

4 When your child feels confident about setting the place, get him to set it off the sheet. Turn the sheet over and out of reach, and when he has completed the setting, he can go back and check to see if he was correct.

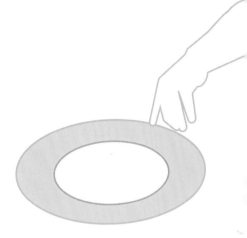

Also try

Add extra items like a glass or a soup spoon and draw on the outlines. You can also add a napkin, but don't draw on the outline—just show how it folds under the fork.

LEARNING TO USE CLOTHESPINS

This activity is one of the simplest ways to help a child develop muscular coordination. It can be achieved by the youngest of children. Once your child has mastered this skill with standard-size clothespins, she can try this activity using mini or toy clothespins. If you have bought new standard clothespins, use them several times to weaken the spring. Explain that clothespins are not toys and should not be applied to fingers as they can pinch and hurt.

You will need

- **Small basket filled with clothespins**

Activity

1 With the basket in front of you, slowly start to attach the clothespins around the basket rim.

2 Demonstrate the opening and closing action of the clothespin so your child will understand that the clothespin must be fully opened to fit onto the basket and to be taken off it again.

3 When you have attached about five clothespins, pass the basket to your child to complete.

4 When she has finished, show her how to remove the clothespins and put them back in the basket.

Also try

The next time you are hanging out some laundry, give some small items of clothing to your child to hang up.

USING TONGS

Children find this activity very appealing as it satisfies their love of sorting and order. The emphasis in this activity is on the opening and closing action, beginning with large tongs and later refining the action using tweezers. Once your child has mastered this activity you can develop it further by asking him to sort the objects by color or shape. Please always supervise your child during this activity as small beads can be a choking hazard or can be inserted into the nose or ears.

You will need

- 2 shallow dishes
- Tongs
- Small tray
- Wooden beads to half-fill one dish

Emphasize the opening and closing movement of the tongs so that your child understands that it is this action that allows the beads to be lifted and moved.

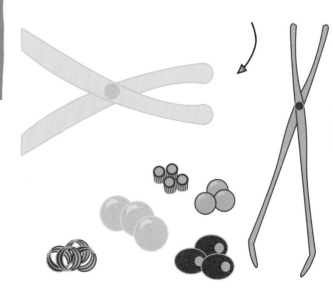

Activity

1 Put the dishes on the tray side-by-side with the tongs on your right. Half-fill the left dish with the beads.

2 Use the tongs (the hand can be held over or under the tongs) to transfer the beads left to right until the left dish is empty.

3 Swap the dishes over so that the dish with the beads is back on the left. Pass the tray over for your child to try.

Also try

Provide two or more empty dishes. Teach your child to transfer between the dishes.

Try the same activity but encourage sorting by object, color, or both.

Use tweezers to transfer dried peas from egg cup to egg cup. This activity uses the same action as tongs, but as it is refined, it is more difficult.

OPENING AND CLOSING OBJECTS

As a child, one of my favorite toys was a miniature toy safe that had a combination lock with a code that only I knew. Today, the children I teach are equally curious about the opening and closing of objects, from the twisting action of a jar's lid, to the turning action of a key in a lock. This activity satisfies that curiosity with opening jars and bottles, similar to the nuts and bolts activity on page 112. Let your child know that the bottles and jars in the basket are available to work with, but that other bottles are out of bounds unless she has been given permission.

You will need

- 6 or more small bottles and jars (for example, food coloring bottles and jam jars)
- Basket

Choose a wide range of bottles and jars so that your child can clearly see the different sizes of openings and lids.

Activity

1 Remove the bottles and jars from the basket. Unscrew all the lids and place them randomly in front of the bottles and jars, neatly in a row.

2 Select a lid and go along the row, left to right, to find the matching bottle or jar. Emphasize the turning action as you find the right match.

3 Repeat until you have done half the bottles or jars and then invite your child to complete the rest.

4 When she has finished, show her how to unscrew the lids. Be very clear about the different turning actions that are used for the opening and closing action. When finished, return everything to the basket.

Also try

Use a range of boxes to show a lifting and shutting action.

Use large, loose nuts and bolts to show a more refined turning action. Supervise closely as nuts could be a choking hazard. See activity on page 112.

USING KEYS

This is an activity that requires deep concentration in children and encourages stillness while their fine motor skills are being put to the test. This exercise teaches coordination, strength, and tests their ability to discriminate by size and remember which key fits in which lock.

You will need

- Gather any bike locks, padlocks, or safes with locks that you have on hand, and their keys
- Tray
- Dish in which to put the keys

Also try

If you don't have any padlocks on hand, you can use your front door and your set of keys. Sit down in front of the door on the inside, so you don't risk getting locked out!

Activity

1   Bring all your locks and padlocks to the tray and lay them all out.

2   Remove all the keys from each lock and place them in a dish.

3   Pick up the first lock in your left hand. Demonstrate how to pick up a key in your right hand and try it in the lock. The first time, use a key that you know will not fit the lock and show how you use a process of eliminiation to find the correct key.

4   When you have found the correct key for the lock, show your child how to turn the key inside the lock the right way until the lock is released.

5   Encourage your child to repeat the process.

6   Once you have matched and unlocked all the locks, show your child how to relock them.

7   Get your child to repeat the locking process until all the keys are released.

THREADING BUTTONS

The activity of threading appeals to all children and is excellent for muscular development and hand–eye coordination. It follows a progression from large buttons with big holes, to small buttons and beads. Once mastered, this skill can be used in jewelry-making and other craft projects. Please always supervise your child during this activity as buttons and small beads can be a choking hazard or can be inserted into the nose or ears.

You will need

- **Selection of large buttons with large holes**
- **Shoelace or piece of string**
- **Small container for buttons**

Activity

1   Put the buttons and the shoelace or a piece of string in the container.

2   Take the shoelace out of the box. Show and explain to your child that you need to knot the end of the shoelace to stop the buttons from sliding off.

3   Slowly thread the buttons, one by one, all the way to the end of the lace. Show clearly the end of the lace

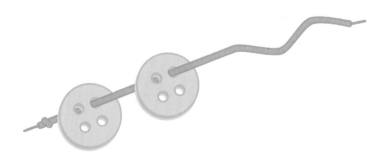

going through the hole, so your child understands that this needs to happen for the button to slide down.

4. Thread about six buttons onto the shoelace and then slide them off and put them back in the container, along with the shoelace.

5. Pass the container over for your child to try. When your child has completed the threading, she may like to have it tied together to make a necklace.

Also try

Replace the buttons with beads, starting with large beads before progressing to smaller beads.

Try using penne pasta. Afterward, color it by dipping the whole necklace in diluted food coloring. See activity on page 104.

SEWING CARDS

In this activity, your child progresses to sewing, using a shoelace, threaded through precut holes around the parameters of sewing cards. Once this skill has been achieved, your child can try sewing with a needle using binka, a fabric with large, precut sewing holes. Sewing is an excellent skill for developing hand–eye coordination. Your child should be aged five or above before he attempts to use a sewing needle. Always supervise closely.

You will need

- Square of cardboard 8 x 8 in. (20 x 20 cm)
- Hole punch
- Scissors
- Pencil
- Shoelace or piece of string
- Markers
- Small tray

Activity

1   Before you sit down with your child, draw an animal shape on the cardboard (make it as large as possible).

2   Cut out the shape and use the pencil to mark off points for the holes at ¾ in (2 cm) intervals. Cut out

holes large enough for the shoelace or
string to fit through easily.

3   Ask your child to color in the card,
    adding a face and animal features. Put
    the sewing card on a tray along with
    the shoelace or string.

4   Show your child what happens when
    you don't make a knot, and then make
    a knot in the shoelace.

5   Pick up the shoelace with one hand
    and begin the sewing action. Start with
    the shoelace above the card, and go
    under. Then bring the shoelace back up
    through the next hole.

6   Go about halfway around and then
    invite your child to complete it. If your
    child would like to repeat the activity,
    remove the shoelace carefully.

Also try

Make a whole set of animal
sewing cards with your child.

Use binka fabric available from
sewing and knitting stores. It is
excellent for introducing needle
sewing as it has large precut needle
holes. Show your child how to use
a knitter's or mending needle, as
these are blunt at the end and have
a large eye.

Introduce your child to colored
threads and stitches, such as
running stitch and cross stitch.

CUTTING WITH SCISSORS

Most children find that to cut a strip of paper in two is relatively simple, but to cut with care and control is another matter. This activity teaches cutting along a marked straight line, using the scissors carefully and moving the paper as you cut. It progresses with cutting more difficult lines and, finally, moving the scissors and paper in different directions. All activities involving scissors need to be supervised closely and the dangers of misusing scissors need to be explained to your child. If your child uses scissors inappropriately, remove them and reintroduce them at a later date.

You will need

- **Child's scissors (left-handed if your child is left-handed)**
- **Ruler**
- **Letter-size sheet of stiff paper**
- **Container to put the strips of paper in**
- **Marker**

Activity

1   Before you ask your child to sit down, cut the paper into five strips widthwise. Mark a straight line down the center of each strip, using the ruler and marker. Put the strips in the container along with the scissors.

2 Pick up the scissors and show your child how to hold them. (Because of your child's smaller hand size, she will probably prefer to put two fingers into the finger hole.) Show your child the opening and closing action of the scissors.

3 Select a strip of paper and hold it in one hand. Cut slowly, following the line.

4 Move the paper along as you are cutting so your child will understand how this helps the cutting process. Exaggerate the opening and closing action so your child will see that this needs to happen if the paper is to be cut. Then cut another strip.

5 Put the scissors back into the container and pass over to your child. Invite your child to finish the rest. From cutting straight lines, your child can progress to wavy lines, zigzags, and castellated lines.

Also try

Provide templates to cut out—for example, animals or vehicles.

Make paper chains. Fold a strip of paper in a concertina fold; draw on a person, making sure that the hands and feet are touching the folds. Ask your child to cut out the figure, but not the hands and feet on the folded edge. When she has finished, open up the paper to reveal the linked people.

MY FAMILY AND FRIENDS

Family and friends are very important to young children, not only in the social sense but also as a means of identifying themselves and their place in the world. This next activity will help your child to establish who her family members are and where they fit in, in relation to her.

You will need

- Photographs of members of your family and of your extended family
- Child's scissors
- Pencil
- Marker
- Template 1 (see page 176), you may need more than one
- Sheets of 8.5 x 11 in. paper
- Glue stick
- Crayons, pencils, or colored markers
- Large sheet of paper to stick the houses onto

Photocopy the template on page 176 onto letter paper. You may like to make multiple photocopies, so that there are enough windows for all your child's extended family members.

Activity

1 Set out the photographs of just the immediate family, scissors, pencil, and marker.

2 Invite your child to come and join you.

3 Explain to her that she is going to make a house with all the members of the family in it.

4 Let her select one of the photographs.

5 In pencil, mark a circle around the photograph so that it will fit in one of the windows of the house.

6 If she is able, let her trace around the pencil circle with the marker.

7 Start cutting around the circle and then, if she is able, let her complete it.

continues on page 168 ➡

8 Repeat steps 4 to 7 with another photograph until all the immediate family photographs have been cut out.

9 Take the photocopy of the house and let your child select one of the photographs.

10 Explain to her that she needs to choose which window she would like to stick the photograph in.

11 Once selected, she needs to glue the back of the photo and stick it in the window.

12 Repeat the process until all the photographs have been stuck onto the house.

13 Under each window write the name of the family member in the photograph.

14 Invite your child to color in the picture.

15 Take another photocopy of the house and repeat the above steps but this time use photographs of any grandparents.

This could be an ongoing project done over a period of a week or two.

16 The same can be done on a separate house for any other extended family members like aunts, uncles, cousins, and so on.

17 When all the houses are complete you may like to stick them onto a large sheet of paper, with the immediate family house in the center and all the other houses around it.

18 Draw a connecting line with an arrow from an immediate family member to the related extended family member's house. On the line write, for example, "Grandma and Grandpa's house, we get there by car." As well as the word "car" draw a picture of a car.

19 Continue until all the family members' houses have been connected.

20 At the top of the sheet of paper you may like to write "All my family."

Also try

After having completed all your family you could repeat the same activity, but this time your child could make separate houses to include all her friends.

Draw an extra window if there are not enough, or you could create a garden around the house and put other family members there.

CARING FOR PLANTS

Once children have mastered their own personal care, the next step is to introduce caring in a wider context, which this activity does by appealing to your child's naturally caring nature. You could introduce it by explaining that all living things need water to survive and grow. Your child will be delighted to be given a responsible role; in addition, he will get to practice his pouring skills.

You will need

- Dishpan or shallow bucket
- Small watering can or pitcher
- Small potted plant

This activity is best done after your child has completed the pouring activities.

Activity

1   Explain to your child that today the plants need to be watered.

2   Place the dishpan or bucket on a table along with the watering can or pitcher.

3   Give him the plant and ask him to carry it to the table and place it inside the bowl or bucket.

4   Pat the soil of the plant and invite him to do the same, so he can observe that the soil is dry.

5   Half-fill up the watering can or pitcher with water. Remind him how to hold it and then allow him to water the plant.

6   Let the plant drain and repeat the activity with another plant.

Also try

Once your child has mastered smaller plants, move onto bigger plants that cannot be carried.

If you have a garden he could help water bigger areas.

WORKSHEET 1

Learning height and length Cut out each rod along the dotted lines.

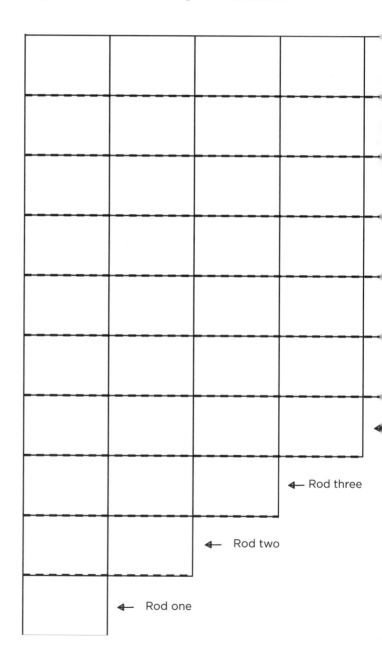

← Rod three

← Rod two

← Rod one

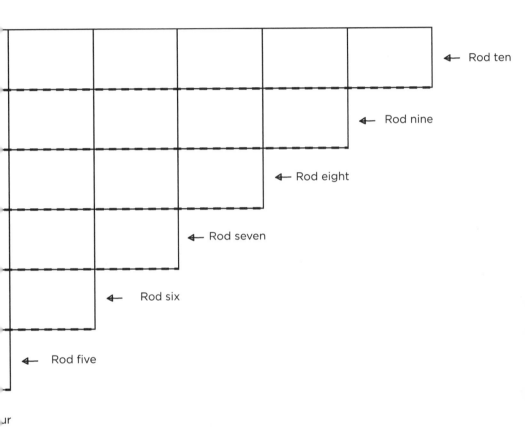

Rod ten

Rod nine

Rod eight

Rod seven

Rod six

Rod five

ur

WORKSHEET 2

Two-dimensional shapes

Matching circles

Matching squares

Matching triangles

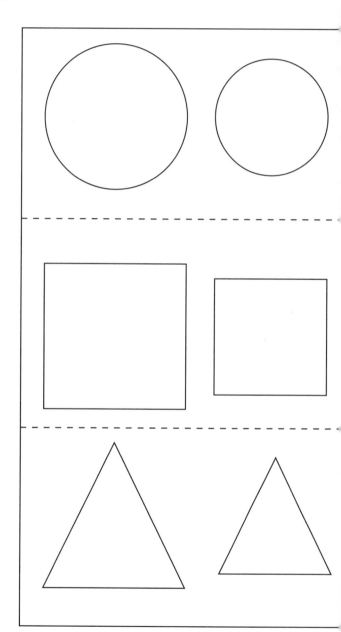

TEMPLATE 1

My family and friends

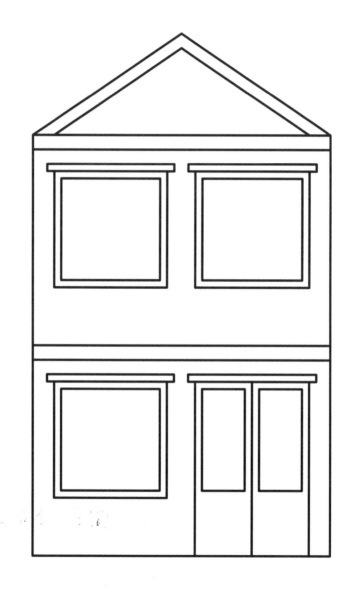